DEERFIELD PUBLIC LIBRARY
920 WAUKEGAN ROAD
DEERFIELD IL 60015-3098

DEERFIELD PUBLIC LIBRARY

3 9094 03129 4604

WITHDRAWN

Doing
Business

Doing Business

the practical guide to **mastering management**

Eric Baron, Michael Benoliel, Wei Hua, Aileen Pincus

Material previously published in
Selling, Negotiating, Presenting

London, New York,
Munich, Melbourne, Delhi

Project Editor: Daniel Mills
Project Designer: Isabel de Cordova
Managing Editor: Penny Warren
Managing Art Editor: Glenda Fisher
Production Editor: Ben Marcus
Senior Production Controller: Man Fai Lau
Creative Technical Support: Sonia Charbonnier
Publisher: Peggy Vance
US Editor: Liza Kaplan

First American Edition, 2011
Published in the United States by
DK Publishing, 375 Hudson Street
New York, New York 10014

11 12 13 14 15   10 9 8 7 6 5 4 3 2 1
178917—January 2011

Copyright © 2008–2009, 2011
Dorling Kindersley Limited. All rights reserved.

Without limiting the rights under copyright
reserved above, no part of this publication may
be reproduced, stored in or introduced into a
retrieval system, or transmitted, in any form, or
by any means (electronic, mechanical, photo-
copying, recording, or otherwise), without the
prior written permission of both the copyright
owner and the above publisher of this book.

Material previously published in: *Presenting,
Negotiating, Selling.*

Published in Great Britain by Dorling Kindersley
Limited. A catalog record for this book is avail-
able from the Library of Congress.
ISBN: 978-0-7566-6860-0

DK books are available at special discounts
when purchased in bulk for sales promotions,
premiums, fund-raising, or educational use.
For details, contact: DK Publishing Special
Markets, 375 Hudson Street, New York,
New York 10014 or SpecialSales@dk.com.

Color reproduction by Alta Images, London
Printed and bound in China by Starlite

Discover more at
www.dk.com

0 3 1 2 9 4 6 0 4

Contents

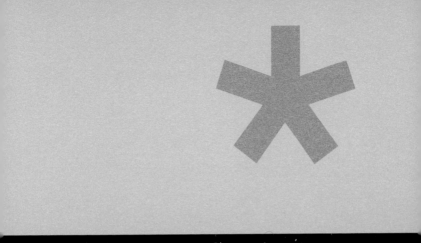

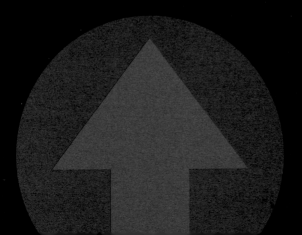

144 PRESENTING

Chapter 1
Planning to present

Chapter 2
Preparing and practicing

Chapter 3
Taking center stage

SELLING

Contents

Introduction

Selling is one of the world's most long-standing professions, and one that constantly moves with, and adapts to, broader changes in business practice, human interactions, and psychology. Selling is also—as every salesperson will tell you—at the cutting edge of every business. Without the eyes, ears, and intuition of a good salesperson, the business itself founders.

Every good salesperson knows his or her products inside and out—whether these are paper clips, aircraft engines, or consultancy services—and can present them capably to customers. However, a great salesperson does much more. He or she understands the customers' needs, and brings a problem-solving mentality and real creativity to their interactions.

Selling is all about combining a set of attitudes, behaviors, and skills in a way that forges long-term relationships with customers—relationships that add value to the customer's business and yield not just one closed deal, but many.

Despite some bad press over the years, selling is an honorable profession. The goal of this book is to open your mind to help you approach selling in a very different way and to introduce the skills you must demonstrate every day. Let the journey begin!

Chapter 1

Building meaningful relationships

People buy from people whom they like, respect, and trust, so selling is really about building and managing relationships. The first step is to find out what your customers expect and demand, and what you need to do to respond accordingly.

Adding value through selling

Offering good products at competitive prices just isn't enough to win sales in today's competitive market. You can bet your best ideas will be emulated by others sooner or later. Today's customers expect you to add value to their business—to address their needs and deliver solutions.

The evolving selling mentality

Being a successful salesperson today requires that you in engage in collaboration, facilitation, and a sense of partnership with your customer. Long gone are the days of one-way persuasion—the canned pitch is considered the lowest level of selling. Ideas about selling have evolved rapidly as globalization and fast communication have produced more savvy and demanding buyers. Selling reflects wider changes in business and today goes far beyond pushing product, embracing an understanding of how organizations work, management structures, psychology, and self-awareness.

TIP

THINK CREATIVELY
Don't limit yourself to thinking only about your products and services—your customers need your creativity to help solve their problems.

Understanding your role

In the past, a salesperson could get by through eloquently telling the customer everything he or she knew about their product, and explaining why their company was the best in its field. This approach may still win you business today in some areas, but most customers now demand much more from their salespeople. They expect them to add value to their business—to understand their needs fully and offer up solutions to problems they didn't even realize they had. To succeed, you have to interpret what the client tells you, and often educate your customer about what's out there. Then you need to mesh together the abilities of your organization with that of the client for the benefit of both. You require a measure of curiosity and good listening skills to uncover what the client really needs. And you must be a brilliant innovator, with the ability to think creatively and manage creative processes that find answers.

 IN FOCUS... SELLING PROFILE

There's no formula for great salespeople—they come from all walks of life and all levels of society. However, they share some characteristics that make them more likely to succeed:
• **Willingness to take risks**—putting their own necks on the line and entering uncharted waters to come up with unique ideas.
• **Generosity**—giving credit to others where deserved without reservation, and sharing credit without fear of diminishing individual contribution.
• **A thick skin**—knowing how to deal with failure, and understanding that even the best lose more often than

they win. With experience, salespeople learn how to deal with inevitable negative responses to their ideas, as well as their own innate emotional responses to setbacks.
• **A methodical approach**—understanding that planning and follow-up are the keys to success.
• **Resourcefulness**—constantly innovating and challenging the existing approaches. Salespeople work well in groups and make the most of the talent around them.
• **Tenacity**—knowing it takes hard work and determination to tackle daunting problems.

Addressing needs

Selling isn't a moment of inspiration; it is not about force of argument or the strength of your personality. It is a process. The process is fairly easy to understand, but—as you'll see—hard to do. The techniques in this book are centered around a process called needs-based selling, so let's examine its principles and set the scene.

TIP

REFRAME THE SALES VISIT

Think of every sales call as a problem-solving opportunity. You are selling more than products and services; you're selling ideas, perspectives, and insights.

Examining the process

The process of selling needs careful planning and management. Beginning a relationship with a new client is the first phase of the process. You can't just walk into a customer's office and kick off a sales meeting. It needs careful staging, and both you and your customer need to be prepared.

Next, you start the most important part of the sales process—determining the customer's needs. During this phase, you ask the key questions, listen to what the customer has to say, identify both the obvious and less obvious needs, enter into a meaningful dialogue, and review what you have learned. Needs determination drives everything in selling, and it is only once you have listened to your customer that you move on to the phase of the process most salespeople enjoy the most: presenting their products and services. This is when you get to explain how you and your company can address your customer's needs. You know your products and services inside and out, and your customers want to hear how you can help them.

Once you have determined the needs and made recommendations, it is time to think about gaining commitment. But something almost always gets in the way—and you face resistance to commit. The customer needs to be allowed to object—even when they seem ready to buy—and you must resolve the client's objections if you are to close the sale.

Needs-based selling

Simply put, needs-based selling means determining a customer's needs before you start to propose solutions. Get to know the customer by letting them speak—at length, if necessary. When it's time to present, you'll do a better job than those who merely display their products and services and you'll be far better positioned to sustain a long-term relationship with your customer.

Solving problems

Success in selling is linked to effective problem solving. If you're good at one, the chances are that you'll excel at the other. The process of problem solving is also remarkably similar in its structure to that of selling (see below), further reinforcing the link.

COMPARING PROBLEM SOLVING WITH SELLING		
STEP	**PROBLEM SOLVING**	**NEEDS-BASED SELLING**
1	Set the stage. Provide structure for the problem-solving session.	Open the meeting. Build rapport, confirm the agenda, prepare the customer.
2	Define the problem. Review background information and solutions already tried.	Determine needs. Engage with the client and tease out both their obvious and their hidden needs.
3	Generate ideas. Provide the climate where everyone can contribute creative perspectives without judgment.	Present products and services. Describe the features and benefits of what you have to sell. Impart your enthusiasm and belief in your products.
4	Evaluate the ideas and develop the best ones. Identify the appealing aspects of an idea, then list the concerns.	Resolve objections. Effectively and sensitively resolve the objections that customers inevitably raise.
5	Summarize the solution. Put together a specific action plan.	Close the deal. Agree on how to move forward with fulfillment.

Appealing to buyers

Countless studies have addressed the central questions of sales—why do buyers buy? How do customers make decisions? What do they demand from salespeople? The answers come down to three discernible behaviors: believing in your position, empathy, and trust.

 TIP

SET THE TONE
You don't have to be funny to be successful in sales, but it helps to be fun. Be the kind of person who brightens up a room when they enter, as opposed to the person who brightens up a room when they leave it.

Establishing your position

People buy from people who know their stuff. If the salesperson can't consistently demonstrate he or she knows what they are talking about, it becomes almost impossible to buy from them.

Put yourself in the buying role. You want to buy a new refrigerator, but the salesperson just can't explain why model A is better for you than model B. Chances are you'll shut down as a customer. In fact, you'll probably want to leave and go to a different store. Knowing what you sell inside-out is a given, but your credibility extends far beyond product knowledge. You must become familiar with your customer's business, competitors, industry, and marketplace. You need to be well prepared. It's not hard—almost everything you need to know about your customers and markets is readily available online.

✓ CHECKLIST GAINING RESPECT BY SHOWING RESPECT

	YES	NO
• Do you show respect for your client's space by, for example, avoiding placing objects on their desk?	☐	☐
• Do you show respect for their business by, for example, asking before you take notes?	☐	☐
• Do you show respect for your competitors? If you put down one of the client's existing suppliers, you are disrespecting the client.	☐	☐

Showing empathy

Empathy is the ability to connect with someone—to see things from their perspective. Several recent studies indicate that, for many buyers, a salesperson's ability to understand their situation is the single most compelling reason why they make the decision to buy.

Many people think empathy depends on similarity of age, background, experience, or point of view. That's a myth. A young salesperson can connect with and relate to someone much more senior if they can identify areas of mutual interest. It's not hard to find common ground. For starters, both are already in the same business—even if they are on different sides of the desk. They may have similar interests and educations: if salespeople allow the customer to talk and genuinely show interest in what they say, the customer will appreciate the empathy they show.

Without understanding the customer and showing real interest in what he or she has to say, a key ingredient in the relationship will be missing and the salesperson will remain an order taker… at best.

GET IN TOUCH

Focus on empathy. Management guru David Maister famously said: "Customers don't care how much you know until they know how much you care."

Building trust

Trust takes a long time to build, but only a second to lose. To demonstrate that you can be trusted, you need to be responsive, direct, clear, reliable, and straightforward. Customers don't like to be manipulated and don't appreciate evasiveness. If you get caught being dishonest in any way, you'll not only lose that customer, but the ripple effect of your actions will spread far beyond the borders of that relationship.

Always assume your customer is smart and give them due respect: don't play games; make sure to deliver on your promises; and don't be the cause of nasty surprises. Follow these simple rules and your customer's trust will follow in time.

Ways to mitigate risk and build trust

START SMALL
Don't ask for all the business; ask for a piece of it. Show the customer your capabilities and earn the business over time.

IDENTIFY PARALLEL SITUATIONS
Review a similar situation with the customer and demonstrate how it worked previously.

Managing risk

You know you are trustworthy, and your customer thinks you are trustworthy. Good start. Being considered trustworthy and actually being trusted to fulfill a million-dollar contract are two different things. US consulting firm Synectics® Inc. carried out some inspired research that accounts for the difference between these two concepts. It is summarized in the trust formula:

$$\text{trust} = \frac{\text{credibility} \times \text{intimacy}}{\text{risk}}$$

The formula shows that your ability to demonstrate credibility and build relationships is directly proportional to trust. But trust is inversely proportional to the level of risk involved in making a decision—how much the client has to lose. The top of the equation is within your control. To be successful in sales, you need to demonstrate credibility (see above) and intimacy, which is comprised of behaviors such as empathy, affability, sensitivity, and likeability. Intimacy speaks to how safe and secure it is to work with you.

So it's the lower part of the equation—risk—that's less within your control and works against your ability to build relationships. To be successful, you must learn to manage risk effectively.

With that in mind, you as a salesperson must constantly ask yourself what you can do to make any commitments less risky for the customer. Remember the old adage: "Nobody ever got fired for hiring IBM." That's because the risk was much lower in hiring Big Blue than a less-established high-tech company.

BUILD IN AN EXIT STRATEGY
Let the customer know there will be a way to get out of the situation if things don't work out as planned.

REASSURE THE CUSTOMER
Tell them you'll be there throughout the process; if anything goes awry you'll be ready to take action if necessary.

EXPLAIN THE WORST CASE
Make the client aware of all the risks and how you'll do your best to keep them under control.

TAKE THE BURDEN
Stand behind what you are doing for the customer; let them know you will take full responsibility if things go wrong.

SHARE THE RISK
Enlighten the customer about the risk for you—if things don't happen as anticipated you'll pay a price as well. Convey that "we're in it together."

GUARANTEE RESULTS
Or at very least, guarantee your commitment to stick together throughout the process.

Differentiating yourself

Whether you're selling computer support, pharmaceuticals, or plumbing supplies, the chances are your competitors offer similar products at equal or better prices with identical backup. You need to do everything to set your product apart from the others, and there is no better way to differentiate your company than through your approach to your customer.

Providing more than the goods

To be a success in sales, you should constantly ask yourself what you can do to add value to the client relationship. If all you do is facilitate the supply of products and services, you are not adding value—just reacting. Even when you provide solutions to known problems, you are still in reactive mode and are not adding much value. This begins only when you help the customer determine their needs.

The goal is to move up the value chain to become a strategic adviser to your customer—someone the customer calls for guidance, ideas, perspective, insights, and, quite simply, help. Once you rise to that level with a customer, your position is rock solid.

BE FIRST

Do whatever you can to keep yourself on the customer's mind, by emailing or sending personal notes and letters. Your customers don't think about you as much as you think about them, so make sure they think of you first when the opportunity arises. But beware—don't become annoying.

Achieving visibility

Make yourself visible to your customer. To rise to the level of a trusted adviser and differentiate yourself from your competition, visit your customers in person on a regular basis. This approach has many benefits: it strengthens the relationship with your customer; it gives you an opportunity to learn their needs directly and through nonverbal clues; and it enables you to see for yourself who your customer regularly interacts with in their organization and the many facets of their work life that remain hidden on the phone.

Surprising your customers

Aim to give your customers something they did not ask for or expect. Let them know you care a bit more than anyone else, you are willing to do things others haven't even thought about, and you are not just concerned about getting the sale. Tom Peters, the world-renowned customer-service guru, talks about "wowing and delighting customers." Showing them you are different can be what ultimately tips the scales in your favor when you and your competitor are running neck and neck.

? ASK YOURSELF... AM I "WOWING" MY CUSTOMER?

- Are there any relevant articles or pieces of research you could send them?
- Can you put them in touch with a third party who can provide something you can't?
- Do you know of any suppliers who could help them reduce their costs?
- Can you help them solve a pressing problem?
- Is there a significant personal event you could acknowledge?
- Do you know someone who is looking to change careers whom they might like to meet?

Chapter 2

Understanding the needs of customers

Almost every sales professional worth his or her salt acknowledges the key importance of understanding their customers' needs. But what does this really mean, and how do you achieve it in the real world?

Implementing the model

The concept of needs-driven or needs-based selling is nothing new. Corporations have always boasted about their ability to develop products that address their customers' needs, and the concept has been incorporated into sales training programs for decades. Why then, is needs-based selling often so poorly implemented?

PRACTICE YOUR SKILLS

When you are in nonbusiness situations with friends or family, ask yourself what their needs are relative to your discussion. It helps you become better at identifying needs and can make you a better friend.

Breaking the 80/20 rule

"Do you understand all of your customers' needs?" In surveys, more that 80 percent of salespeople answer "yes" to this question. Yet studies of their customers reveal that, seen from the client's side, only 20 percent of salespeople are addressing needs. Some people call this startling discrepancy in perceptions the "80/20 rule." As a salesperson, you need to understand why this happens, and what you can do to make sure you're part of the successful 20 percent.

TIP

QUESTION YOURSELF

Think of something you bought recently. Why did you buy it? What need did you have? How did the product address it? How effective was the salesperson you bought it from? Ask yourself questions like this and your understanding of customers' needs will become clearer.

Taking your time

So why is it that so many salespeople respond in a way that their clients don't want? The answer is—in part—they are too eager. Early in a sales meeting, they hear a need from a customer and, with the best of intentions, start to address it, start to provide a solution. You are probably thinking: "Isn't that what needs-driven selling is all about?" Not exactly: if you hear a need and respond to it immediately, it's a little like reading the first chapter of a book and drawing conclusions regarding the author's message. You know a bit—but only that; the whole story awaits. Any premature recommendation is likely to miss the mark, resulting in a disappointed customer.

It takes a lot of self-confidence to step back and admit to yourself and your client that you're not yet prepared to make a recommendation. You need to acknowledge you don't understand your customer as well as you thought and that you need to ask more questions. This level of humility doesn't come naturally to most salespeople.

? ASK YOURSELF...
HOW DO I TUNE IN TO A CLIENT'S NEEDS?

Each time you interact with a customer, ask yourself these types of questions to put yourself in the right mindset:

• What is this person trying to accomplish?
• What does he or she really want from me?
• What are their primary concerns?
• What's holding them back?
• What are they getting/not getting from their current supplier(s)?
• What gaps exist in their current relationship(s)?
• Why are they taking the time to see me?

Seeing the nature of needs

Before you start questioning your customer to uncover their needs, it helps to know what these needs might look like—and how they are likely to present themselves. You'd be surprised at how even the most seasoned sales professionals have difficulty recognizing needs.

TIP

ANALYZE YOUR THOUGHT PROCESS

Whenever you find yourself offering a solution to a customer, ask yourself what the need is that led to this solution. You'll be amazed at how taking one step back will leave you two steps forward.

Separating needs from solutions

The respected Harvard economist Theodore Levitt famously said: "Nobody needs a drill, they need a hole." In other words, people's real needs are sometimes hidden behind apparent solutions.

A simple example may help illuminate what Levitt was getting at. Imagine you own a travel agency. A customer walks in days before the winter vacation; he's in a panic because he hasn't arranged that big vacation he promised his wife and children. You listen patiently. He says the family is so excited, but he's worried that he's left the arrangements too late. He tells you the vacation is hard to plan because his three children have such different interests—from going to museums to rock climbing—while his wife just needs to have some down time. He brags about how the cost issue is not a big deal to him.

CASE STUDY

New blood for Citibank

In the early 1980s, Citibank was one of the first major financial organizations to attempt the creation of a unique sales culture. The Consumer Banking Group interviewed many of the largest sales training companies, but—to the surprise of many—hired a young, small, and virtually unknown firm to lead the charge. When the decision-maker was asked why she chose that firm, her response was simple: "Of all the firms we interviewed, they did the best job of demonstrating they understood our needs. And if that's what we want to teach our people, let's go with people who practice what they preach." Enough said.

TIP

SELLING BLANKS

Approach some sales calls as if you were "selling without a product." This forces you to focus strictly on the customer—a productive habit to get into.

When salespeople hear stories like this, many immediately start thinking up solutions. "What can we offer him that will address all his issues? If he wants to spend more, let's help him—it's more more commission for us. 'What your family needs, sir, is a spa vacation in Miami.'"

This might indeed be a satisfactory solution, but the salesperson has done little to understand the customer's needs. A little analysis, and further questioning, might reveal the client has a need to impress and be respected by his family; to act quickly; to carve out some adult time on his vacation; to have a safe, supervised environment; and many other needs besides. Taking this longer approach has real benefits: the customer feels understood and valued; he'll buy this vacation from you, and come back for your guidance and advice, year after year.

"My family can't agree on what kind of vacation we should take."

"Katie and Mike love sports but Jack is much happier exploring, and Susan just wants to relax."

"I know I've left it late, but it has to be something that keeps both my kids and my wife happy."

"No problem. Let's start by exploring what you need a little further. What were the best things about your last vacation?"

TIP

BE SENSITIVE
After each meeting, ask yourself what the customer didn't say. You'll probably unearth some needs they did not consciously know they had.

Reading between the lines

Sometimes your customers will tell you exactly what they need. All you have to do is listen and respond. But if you address only these overt needs, you are not adding much value to the client, and you are doing no more than any of your competitors would do. Where you can differentiate yourself—and win the client's respect and trust—is by hearing and responding to implied needs. So your task is to look for the needs behind what the customer says. For example, if the client complains about his boss constantly second-guessing him, he may be expressing a need to have a solid, tightly reasoned explanation for his buying decisions. Successful sales professionals know how to uncover these implicit needs—indeed, it is what drives their long-term success.

Selling would be a far easier task if customers could be relied on always to buy for sound business reasons, such as return on investment, quality, value, and competence. If the buyer always made his or her decision dispassionately, rather than based on how that decision made them feel, reading their requirements would be straightforward.

BUSINESS AND PERSONAL NEEDS

Business needs are measurable while personal needs are subjective. Below are some examples of each to illustrate the differences between the two.

BUSINESS NEEDS	PERSONAL NEEDS
Reduce cost	Look good in front of peers
Increase efficiency	Gain recognition
Shorten production time	Get that promotion
Become more effective	Minimize the risk
Increase profitability	Boost personal status
Improve turnaround time	Decrease stress

However, all customers—however company-focused they may be—are to some extent influenced by personal needs. These delve into areas that are harder to quantify—security, connecting with others, ego, and comfort. For this reason, showing empathy with the customer will bring you rich rewards.

Beginning the questioning

Before you begin to question your client to determine their needs, let them know why you need the information, how it will benefit them, and how it relates to the agenda. Explain that by answering your questions they will:

- Help you focus on the right issues
- Allow you to make better recommendations
- Get an opportunity to outline their concerns
- Make sure that you learn about them.

They are more likely to be open and honest with their answers if they understand the structure of the needs determination process (see right).

Asking, and asking again

Many pieces of research on the selling process point to one simple conclusion: the more questions you ask of your client, the more success you'll enjoy because the person who learns the most needs is primed to win the business. But the corollary is that the longer you manage a relationship, the more likely you are to lose sales. That is because, over time, you become complacent, making assumptions about the customer rather than asking questions. That's why many salespeople report a falling share of sales, just when they thought the relationship was thriving. The bottom line is to keep asking questions consistently, methodically, and creatively.

HOW TO... FIND OUT CLIENT NEEDS

Introduce the questioning session

↓

Ask the right questions

↓

Listen for the needs

↓

Review and check the needs

TIP

RECOGNIZE MOTIVES

Watch out for customers who are risk averse, or who appear to worry about how they are going to appear; they tend to be driven more by personal needs.

Planning your approach

Most sales managers agree that the margins separating good, very good, and excellent salespeople are not dependent on what happens face-to-face, but what happens before and after the sales process. You may feel energized and ready to jump straight into a sales meeting with a new customer, but if you spend time planning the content and thinking through the process, your chances of success will be greatly enhanced.

Doing your homework

The first stage of planning is getting your content right—ensuring you have all the information you need for every stage of the sales process.

Start your preparation by determining the objectives of the meeting, both for you and the customer. Once these are established, ask yourself what you already know about the customer and what you still need to learn. There is no excuse for not knowing what is going on in your customer's industry and marketplace. There are many sources of data you can investigate to make sure you are prepared, including (but not limited to) annual reports, product brochures, articles, press clippings, industry magazines, and trade show summaries. Check out your customer's website and try

Questions to prepare you for the sales meeting

Who?
- Who makes the decisions?
- Who should I see?
- Who will do what from our side?

What?
- What questions will I ask?
- What drives this customer's decisions?
- What ideas will I suggest?
- What objections do I anticipate?

to get a sense of what changes are on the horizon in their business. Find out about their competitors, pay attention to what the marketplace is saying, and understand what your customers are demanding.

If appropriate, think about what you want to recommend to the customer, and the corresponding features and benefits. Try to anticipate objections, and ask yourself what the real issues might be and what answers you may be able to provide.

Preparing the process

Getting the content right is important, but you also need to plan how to manage the selling process—the way you deliver the information. Consider all the stages of the selling process, from opening the meeting to closing the deal. Do you know what you will do and say in each one and how you will manage the transitions between the phases? Feeling relaxed and well prepared is crucial, so rehearse your presentation repeatedly, and ask for feedback from colleagues. Practice delivering your questions, resolving objections, and even closing. This will highlight any areas in which you are less than confident, and reveal any holes in the information you need to succeed.

Where and when?
- Where is the best place to conduct the meeting?
- When would be the most effective time?

Why?
- Why is this approach good for our business?
- Why are we targeting this specific customer?

How?
- How will I run the meeting?
- How can I differentiate us from our competitors?

Making your first move

It has lots of names—the initial contact, the cold call, the first call, the canvas, the exploratory call, and others. That first visit to a prospective customer can be a daunting, even scary, experience for most people early in their careers. The good news is that this does change over time.

HOW TO... MAKE INITIAL IMPACT

Get the lead

↓

Write your letter of introduction

↓

Make the call and secure an appointment

↓

Confirm the appointment in writing

↓

Make the initial visit

↓

Send a follow-up letter

Finding the way in

You can't set up a first meeting until you have a lead. Experiment with finding different sources of leads:

- Former customers
- Referrals from existing customers
- Newspaper articles and industry publications
- Trade shows/symposiums
- The "dead file"—prospects others have given up on
- Centers of influence (third parties).

Armed with leads, your key prospecting tool will be the letter. You can justify three of these in the prospecting process: one to introduce yourself; one to confirm an appointment to meet; and one to follow up the initial meeting. Emails are fine once you have a relationship, but send a traditional letter for the initial approach—it will set you apart from the competition.

Making an appointment

In some industries, it can be acceptable just to drop by, but regardless of the business you are in, you will be more successful if you obtain an appointment first. Send a confirmation letter, letting the customer know you are looking forward to meeting them and confirm the date, time, and time allocation. Review your own agenda and include some relevant material for the customer to look at. Encourage them to invite anyone who might benefit from attending.

Creating an impression

Your first meeting with a new prospect may have many purposes—from a simple introduction to a full-blown sales call. Whatever happens, stay calm and begin the process of understanding your potential customer's needs. You should try not to present anything specific (although you should be prepared to present your company's credentials, see the following page). Instead, establish rapport, and let the customer do most of the talking.

Learn what you can about the individual and their business. Look for, and reinforce, common ground. Are they familiar with your company? Is there any relevant history between your organizations that could form a bond? Do you share interests or acquaintances in the industry?

HAVE FUN

Try thinking of cold calls as fun. You'll never know exactly what to expect, so be ready for anything and take pride in your ability to respond to the situation. It's a new beginning—be sure to make it a memorable one.

MAKING THE FIRST VISIT

FAST TRACK	OFF TRACK
Confirming the meeting in writing to show interest	Just showing up without putting in the preparation time
Being humble—you haven't been there before	Showing unfounded familiarity—it's only the first meeting
Doing your homework and demonstrating what you have learned in preparation for the visit	Treating this meeting as if it were just like any other meeting
Showing appreciation for the customer taking the meeting	Behaving as if you are entitled to be there
Asking lots of questions of the customer and letting them talk	Presenting specific recommendations

Presenting your credentials

Despite your best intentions to focus on the customer's needs, you will often find you are asked to give a quick explanation of who you are and what you have to offer—a credentials presentation—before the customer will give you any information about themselves.

Aiming for needs first

A credentials presentation is an overview of your company, what it does, and how it adds value to its customers. You need to be prepared to give a brief presentation, but if you can avoid having to do so at this early stage of your relationship with a customer, you should—as soon as you start talking about how to help them before identifying and confirming their needs, it becomes more about you than about them. If your customer opens with: "Tell me about your company," it can sometimes work to respond with: "I'll be delighted to explain who we are and how we may be of assistance, but I can do that much more effectively if I learn a bit about you first." If the customer agrees, you can start the needs-determination process; if not, you will have to make a credentials presentation.

TIP

KEEP IT GENERAL
Use the presentation to give a brief overview of needs you can fulfill and your product line. Don't make assumptions about your customer's needs or offer a particular product or service.

"Our products address a range of needs"

Getting the message right

A good way to build a credentials presentation is to use your team—not just the sales team, but anyone in the business who would like to contribute. Ask different members of the team to put themselves in the position of a customer of your company, and talk to you about what they would like to hear. As you build your presentation, practice it with the team. Discuss how it sounds and adjust it until you get it right.

The key to a successful credentials presentation is to keep it short, focused, and to the point. Don't overload the customer with information—you will (hopefully) have the opportunity to do that later. Give some history about the company and yourself as a way to explain who you are. If you have an interesting anecdote about how the company started, don't be afraid to share it. In a general sense, aim to tell them the kinds of things you do and the kinds of companies you work with, and briefly outline your success stories. Discuss needs in general, and then explain why what you have to offer can be of value to a company like theirs. Again, words like "can," "could," or "might" are more appropriate because you have not yet learned enough about your customer to get specific.

✔ CHECKLIST PREPARING A CREDENTIALS PRESENTATION

	YES	NO
• Have you discussed with your team how you want to position your company to people who aren't familiar with what you do?	☐	☐
• Have you used your company's mission and vision statements to provide key facts and figures?	☐	☐
• Have you trimmed your presentation so it can be delivered within a few minutes?	☐	☐
• Have you practiced in front of a friend or colleague until you are fully confident in your delivery?	☐	☐

Opening a sales meeting

When you make an appointment to see a client—whether it is your first or your fiftieth—you are effectively calling a meeting for that customer. For the meeting to run well, you need to take the initiative, while at the same time acknowledging that the meeting belongs to the customer—it must be focused on providing solutions to their problems.

Building rapport

What happens in the first few minutes of a sales visit sets the tone for the entire meeting. It helps break the opening down into three critical steps: building rapport, confirming the agenda, and moving into the meeting itself.

At the start of the meeting, make sure everyone is comfortable, knows who is who, and has a chance to connect informally. Encourage small talk or a discussion of general business conditions. Use your intuition to decide when to move on—you need to work at your customer's comfort level, not your own. Here are a few ideas to help you get off to a good start:

• Look around the client's office for something to trigger conversation, such as a picture or trophy.
• Compliment the customer on their office or facility—but you must be sincere.
• Thank the customer for their time.
• Discuss something you know about their business—a relevant news event, for example—to show you've done your homework.

IN FOCUS...
TALKING TO THE RIGHT PERSON

Surprisingly, two-thirds of all sales calls are made to people who do not make or implement decisions. Salespeople are often reluctant to ask a prospect whether they are speaking to the person who is responsible for calling the shots, for fear of sounding disrespectful. The following preamble can help you check if you're talking to the right person: "I visit many organizations like yours and everyone has their own way of making decisions. To ensure that I don't waste anyone's time or leave someone out of the loop, would you please share with me how the process works here?"

Setting the agenda

Next, make sure everyone is clear about the objectives of the meeting. Even though this is a sales call, it requires a clear agenda, distributed in advance, which takes into account your needs and your client's (remember, it is their meeting). Give each person the opportunity to express their interest in the meeting and what they would like to get out of it. This is crucial. You may not realize the status or position of a participant in your meeting, and run the risk of missing out on a huge opportunity.

Finally, confirm the time available for the meeting, and stick to it. Customers resent people who overstay their welcome.

Guiding the meeting

Old-style salespeople hated to lose control of a meeting, and so did all the talking and tried to force the customer onto their agenda. You can see now that this isn't consistent with a problem-solving approach to selling. Instead, you should acknowledge that the meeting belongs to the customer—you are there to solve their problems, after all. Your role is more as facilitator, to make sure the meeting runs smoothly. Once you begin addressing issues on the agenda, make sure the meeting stays focused on the stated purposes. Try to draw out ideas from all participants, then move the meeting toward an action plan, and schedule the follow-up.

Roles in the sales meeting

THE SALESPERSON
- Facilitates the meeting
- May take minutes
- Participates in finding solutions

THE CLIENT
- Owns the problem
- May chair the meeting
- Participates in finding solutions

OTHER PARTICIPANTS
- Participate in finding solutions
- Contribute problem-solving resources

Questioning for needs

Of all the skills demanded of a successful salesperson, questioning remains the most important. This is simply because you can't hope to understand a customer's needs without asking questions in a thoughtful, credible, and sensitive way.

Running the session

When you question a customer at a sales meeting, you need to keep the session light—think of it as an open discussion rather than an interrogation. Comfortable customers invariably reveal more—and more useful—information.

The questions you ask to determine needs fall into three broad categories—fact-finding questions, needs-oriented questions, and big-picture questions— each of which are considered below. There are no hard-and-fast rules about the types of question to ask

CASE STUDY

Asking the right questions

One of the classic stories in the sales business recalls how Pepsi-Cola won the airline business from Coca-Cola in the 1990s. At the time, Coca-Cola owned the in-flight business and there was no way Pepsi could win the business in a price war. The new national sales manager was about to make his first call on one of the airlines and had prepared a lavish and thoughtful presentation. At the last minute, one of his internal resources suggested they show up with only a pad and pen—no presentation at all.

Against his better instincts, he agreed. For two hours, all they did was ask questions and learn about the airline. They hardly mentioned Pepsi. They learned that beyond ensuring safety, the biggest need the airline had was to sell more tickets. They had uncovered a critical requirement they had to meet if they were to be successful in their bid for the business.

They developed a plan to give retailers coupons that allowed them to buy airline tickets at a discount. At the time, this was a unique approach, which departed from the pattern of typical promotions. The airlines loved the idea, awarded Pepsi the business, and in the first year alone were able to sell more than $2 million in additional tickets. A legendary result.

your customer, but experience suggests that a ratio of around five fact-finding questions, to three needs-oriented-questions, and one big-picture question is comfortable for the client and achievable for you.

Finding the facts

To scope out an account or manage a relationship, you need some fundamental pieces of information about the client—their customers, partners, suppliers; their company structure; number of employees; and so on. These questions may seem obvious, but it's surprising how often they are overlooked. These are usually closed questions that can be answered "yes" or "no" or with a fact. Their job is to elicit information, so they tend not to be all that imaginative (virtually everybody asks them), but can be surprisingly provocative (for example, "Who makes the decisions here?"). They are essential but won't do a whole lot to differentiate you from your competition.

Probing the needs

Needs-oriented questions get the customer talking and are far more open-ended. They can be quite imaginative—"If you could change one thing about the way you do business today, what would that be?"—or even provocative. Typically, these questions do not have "right" or "wrong" answers. They open up new areas of discussion, and will absolutely help differentiate you from your competition.

Responses from the customer will encompass everything from their objectives, goals, hopes, expectations, and aspirations to their problems, concerns, worries, and fears. As your relationship with the client evolves, you can ask progressively deeper questions that will help reinforce trust.

TIP

LEARN FROM THE PROS
Watch the great interviewers on television. They ask short questions and don't give the person being interviewed possible answers. They ask a question and stop talking; try the same technique.

Learning about the big picture

Big-picture questions position you to uncover needs the customer does not necessarily know he or she has. They are strategic in nature, in essence asking the customer to think about things they may not like to consider—the future of the business, difficulties to be overcome, the need to plan, contingencies, and long-term goals. Big-picture questions require planning on your part because they can lead to uncomfortable— albeit valuable—discussions. They are necessarily thought-provoking, and will stay in the customer's mind for a long time. They elevate the conversation, and will eventually result in your being perceived as an adviser or consultant— much more than a salesperson.

TIP

BEWARE OF THE WHY?
Be careful of questions that begin with "why." They can appear judgmental and condescending and can put people on the defensive. It helps to introduce these types of questions with a preamble.

Planning the ask

Most people are naturally suspicious of questions. When determining needs, you should be as sensitive as possible during the process of questioning your client.
• Give a preamble: let the customer know that questions are coming, why you are asking, and how it is in their interests to answer.
• Cluster questions into categories, focusing on strategy, finance, inventory, and so on, each with its own preamble.
• Be straightforward in your questions.
• Don't shy away from the tough questions.

Questions to investigate the client's needs

FACT-FINDING
- What are your annual sales?
- Who are your current suppliers?
- How often do you purchase?
- How much do you work with this account?
- Who makes the decisions?

NEEDS-ORIENTED
- What are your expectations of someone like me?
- What changes are you initiating to stay competitive?
- How has globalization impacted your business?
- What are some of the biggest challenges you face today?
- How has your customer base changed?

BIG-PICTURE
- What is your vision for the company?
- Where would you like the company to be in five years?
- What obstacles could prevent that from happening?
- How do you see yourself leveraging your strengths in the long-term?
- How will you make sure that you benefit from globalization?

Listening to your client

You can ask your client brilliantly incisive questions to determine their needs. But these are worth little if you don't listen to their responses. Listening isn't easy—studies reveal that we retain a tiny percentage of what we hear—but it is a critical skill for any salesperson.

ASK FIRST
Always ask if it's OK to take notes and show respect for confidentiality. Clients will rarely decline and will probably be flattered you want to record what they say.

Staying tuned in

As a salesperson, you are the eyes and ears of your organization; what you learn about your client in a sales meeting will make your company stand or fall. You should be listening at a high level all the time— collecting facts, information, and business-related concepts—but most of all, listening for needs. Of course, this is the ideal scenario, and in reality your ability to listen is jeopardized by many factors. Instead of listening, you may start anticipating the next question, planning your response, or trying to understand what the customer meant. You may get distracted thinking about your route home or tomorrow's meetings; and there are biological reasons why attentive listening is harder than it seems—we think much faster than we can talk. But whatever your reason for tuning out, you can be sure that when you do, you're missing vital information.

CASE STUDY

Showing interest

Four out of five clients think that when you don't take notes, you aren't fully engaged. This research is borne out by a story related by a sales manager, who, along with a colleague, began a sales meeting with a prospective client. Neither was taking notes. After a few awkward minutes, the client called his assistant on the phone and said: "Please bring two pads and two pens for our guests as I would like to have the impression that they are at least somewhat interested in what I have to say." This is a true story—don't let this happen to you!

Making notes

There are many ways to enhance your listening skills, of which one of the best known is Active Listening*— a concept that has been around more than half a century and is explored in dozens of courses and books. A simple, and arguably more effective technique can be set out in just two words—Take Notes, or more accurately, Make Notes. From the minute the customer starts talking, you should put pen to paper. The distinction between "making" and "taking" notes is important because you are doing more than just recording the client's words—you are jotting down any connections you make, and capturing on paper the need, the concern, the issue, the opportunity. Don't analyze too much—there will be plenty of time for that later.

The discipline of making notes has further benefits—it stops you from trying to respond too early, and it ensures that you listen to the customer throughout the meeting. It's a fact that many people "save the best for last," revealing their deepest needs toward the end of a conversation. If you present too early, chances are you'll miss hearing vital information.

*Active Listening— a structured form of listening that focuses attention on the speaker. A listener consciously attends fully to the speaker and then repeats in their own words what he or she thinks the speaker has said, often interpreting the speaker's words in terms of feelings.

Approaching a problem

Bringing a problem-solving approach into your dealings with customers has clear benefits. But how do you put it into practice? Problem-solving seems intangible and difficult, but following a structured process, such as the technique of brainstorming, will bring focus to your interactions with customers and increase your chances of sales success.

TIP

MAKE SPACE FOR INNOVATION

Don't overdefine a problem. Usually, if people learn too much about a problem, they will become less willing to speculate and will find themselves putting on the same blinders that the problem owner already has.

Setting the scene

Problem solving requires creativity—but that doesn't mean chaos. When you bring together a group to develop creative solutions, you need to give the meeting structure. Be sure to define the task, decide what approach you will use and how much time is available, and establish who is chairing, facilitating, and taking the minutes of the meeting.

Next, the group should identify the problem and set it into a proper context of background information. Why is the problem a problem? Could it be turned into an opportunity? Has the problem been addressed before, and how? Who is responsible for results? Once the meeting has been staged and the problem defined, the group is ideally positioned to generate ideas through brainstorming.

IN FOCUS... BRAINSTORMING

When it is done correctly, the technique of brainstorming taps people's capacity for lateral thinking and free association and boosts creative output. The concept was conceived in the 1920s by Alex Osborn, partner in international advertising agency BBDO (he was the "O" in the company). Osborn summarized the technique in the statement: "It is easier to tone down a wild idea than to think up a new one." Many precede their brainstorming sessions with creativity or relaxation exercises to help participants move into a more creative state.

Encouraging creative solutions

When you begin a brainstorming session, invite ideas, perspectives, recommendations, and insights. Encourage participants to be speculative and open—the meeting should be energetic, exciting, and fun. Resist any temptation to evaluate ideas as soon as they are put forward—anything goes. The opportunity to be innovative invariably yields richer results than if individuals feel constrained by rules or limitations.

Evaluating results

Brainstorming is a great way to spend the first half of a problem-solving session. The second part must be devoted to selecting the most exciting ideas and evaluating them diligently to develop solutions.

The evaluation process doesn't have to be complex, but it does have to be managed with care. Once an idea has been selected, the challenge becomes how to turn it into a solution.

One of the most common approaches suggests first identifying the appealing aspects of an idea and then listing concerns. Identifying the positives ensures that the parts of the idea you want to save are captured and preserved. Then address each concern, beginning with the most troubling, until the idea becomes acceptable. At this point, when the idea has been transformed into a solution, carefully summarize your conclusions and put together a specific action plan that includes the next steps to implement the results.

Reviewing needs

The perfect way to complete the needs assessment and move into the presentation phase is to demonstrate to the customer that you have been listening, you understand what they have been saying, and you're in tune with what they hope to accomplish.

TIP

SEEK CONFIRMATION

If there are several people in the room, check with each of them that your understanding of the needs matches theirs. Just because one person agrees with you doesn't mean they all do.

Selling before presenting

Everything you have done up to this point has been focused on learning the needs of your customer. But before you start to present your solutions, you should demonstrate a clear understanding of his or her situation. If you review the needs well, you'll demonstate credibility, empathy, sensitivity, and trustworthiness—and many buyers will make their decision to buy at this point, even before you have presented your goods and services. Conversely, without thoroughly reviewing the needs, you risk misunderstanding your client and missing the mark with your recommendations.

CHOOSING YOUR WORDS

FAST TRACK

OFF TRACK

FAST TRACK	OFF TRACK
"Here's my understanding of what you said..."	"What you need is..."
"I may be reading too much into this, but it appears that..."	"You said that..."
"How I interpreted X's statement was that you had a desire to..."	"X told us that you wanted..."

IN FOCUS...
THE PSYCHOLOGY OF LISTENING

Carl Rogers (1902–1987) was one of the world's greatest psychologists and students of human communication. He famously said that the "greatest compliment one human being can pay another is to demonstrate that he was listening." When a sales professional takes the time to review with a customer his or her understanding of that customer's needs, they are indeed paying a great compliment and differentiating themselves—yet again—from the competition in an emphatic manner.

Ensuring a close match

When you begin the review, choose your words carefully—tell the client what you heard as opposed to what they said. The distinction is subtle, but keeps you from putting words in the client's mouth (see box, opposite). Start by summarizing the client's overt needs and move to those you need to infer. Ask the client to confirm your review is correct, and request that they prioritize their needs. Ask if you missed anything, if there's anything they'd like to add, or if your understanding is flawed. You just might pick up another need along the way.

Timing the review

The best time to review needs is either at the end of a needs-determination meeting or at the beginning of a meeting in which you are presenting (especially if new people are present, or a lot of time has passed since the last meeting). Concluding a meeting by reviewing needs ends it on a positive note and sets the stage for the next meeting when you will present. If you have done everything right, the client will already have a strong inclination to buy from you.

Selling with others

Bringing a colleague with you—whether it's your manager, a subject expert, another member of the team, or the new salesperson who just joined the company—can potentially make your sales meeting much more effective. However, joint sales meetings need to be managed carefully if they are to live up to their potential.

TIP

TALK UP YOUR COLLEAGUES

When you introduce your colleagues on a joint call, emphasize why it is important that they have been able to come along. For example: "I'm delighted Susan could join us. She has been working on these kinds of problems for 15 years."

Being prepared

Preparation is the key to effective joint sales meetings. First, anyone you bring with you to the meeting needs to have a full understanding of its objective. At the very least, they need to know who the customer is, what they do, where you are in the relationship, and what you hope to accomplish. Equally importantly, your colleagues need to be clear about what their role in the meeting will be, or you run the risk they will be unprepared. Are they there to ask questions, make recommendations, help deal with objections, or just to show support and interest?

Managing a joint meeting

In a joint sales meeting, it is even more important that you act as the facilitator, managing the process and trying to make sure that the meeting fulfills both your own objectives and your customer's. Get the meeting off to a positive start by inviting introductions. Make sure everyone knows who everyone else is, and that they are clear about what each party hopes to accomplish. During the meeting, it is important that every member of your team makes a contribution, so call on your colleagues when their expertise is needed, and explain why: "I would like John to answer that question because it falls within his area of expertise."

Benefits of joint sales meetings

SPECIALIZED KNOWLEDGE
Inviting colleagues from different functional areas of your organization to join you at the meeting allows you to offer a greater range of expertise to the customer.

LOOKING GOOD
Bringing a team—especially if it includes senior members of your organization—may impress the customer, and make them feel they are important to you.

TWO PAIRS OF EARS
Sales meetings can be fast paced, especially if you are acting as the facilitator. If you have a colleague with you, they can pick up on small details you may miss.

DIFFERENT PERSPECTIVES
With more than one of you interpreting what the customer is saying, you may get a fuller understanding of the customer's needs.

IMPROVING PERFORMANCE
Your colleagues can give you feedback on your performance, enabling you to be even more effective at your next sales meeting.

Chapter 3

Making your recommendations

Providing solutions and making recommendations is the part of the selling process most salespeople like best. It's time to demonstrate how you can help the customer, tell your story, and present your products and services.

Using features and benefits

Client presentations take many forms; they range from informal one-to-one meetings to formal expositions to a conference room full of potential clients. Surprisingly, regardless of the situation, your approach will not vary that much. Your presentation will focus on features and benefits.

Defining the terms

Salespeople have used features and benefits to describe their products and services for many decades. This approach has stood the test of time for one reason—it works!

Features tell customers how products or services work. They are characteristics, descriptions, attributes, specifications, and explanations. Benefits explain how the product helps—why it is important to the client and how it addresses their needs. Benefits set out to the customer the value of the item being discussed and why it is in their interests to purchase it.

Selling the benefits

People make the decision to buy things because of their benefits rather than their features. However, most salespeople are more comfortable talking about features than benefits. It's not hard to see why. Features are facts and hard to debate. You will rarely be challenged when you explain the features of a product or service—they are tangible and objectively notable.

Benefits, on the other hand, are educated guesses. They are subjective—what might be a benefit for one person may not be a benefit for another. Talking about benefits makes some people uncomfortable because it feels like a "hard sell." It shouldn't. Benefits do no more than explain why a recommendation makes sense.

When you make your presentation, think in terms of benefit statements, and always try to link your features to the benefits. If you don't, you're only telling half the story. The example below—where a salesperson presents a new design of conference chair—shows the types of connections to make.

Linking features and benefits

FEATURE OF CHAIR	BENEFIT OF CHAIR
Neat, stackable design	Saves space, making it ideal for even the smallest venues
Metal legs	Durable—has a lifespan twice as long as close competitors, saving money
Stiffened back	Enhanced comfort and better sitting position—ideal for longer conferences
Discreet handle	Easy to carry and reposition—gives more flexibility at the venue.

Targeting the pitch

Features and benefits are the trusted selling tools that address the client's questions "What?" and "So what?" But if you can answer one further question—"What's in it for me?"—you'll set yourself apart from the competition. This question addresses the specific benefit—the particular needs of an individual customer.

TIP

HOLD BACK THE BROCHURE

Try using your sales brochure only after you have presented, not before. Highlight the areas where your products meet the client's needs.

Focusing on specifics

Your ability to express the features and benefits of your products is vital, but there's one more conceptual step to take—understanding and presenting specific benefits. Every customer buys for slightly different reasons. Some base their decisions on quality, convenience, and price; others on the level of service, or personal reasons that reflect how they feel about themselves. Specific benefits speak to the confirmed, most important, needs of a particular client; they differ from generic benefits, which make broader statements about the value of a product or service.

Prioritizing your messages

Information about your products and services and their corresponding features and benefits is fixed information—it's what you might include in your brochure, spec sheet, or catalog. By contrast, the needs of each customer and the specific benefits you present are variable. This variable information is at the heart of the needs-driven selling process—it's what elevates your presentation far above the canned pitch.

So, when the time comes to present, deliver the variable information first. Start by succinctly reviewing the customer's needs. Next, make recommendations and demonstrate how they address the customer's needs—the specific benefits. Only when this is done should you move on to presenting the generic features and benefits. At first glance, this ordering of the information appears backward—going from the specific to the general. However, it addresses the reality of your audience's attention span. High-level listening efficiency lasts a frighteningly short time—up to 90 seconds—before dipping precipitously. Specific benefits are what close deals, so be sure to get them in early, before your client's attention wanders.

HOW TO... ORDER YOUR PITCH

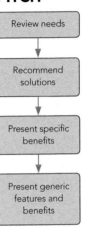

IN FOCUS... THE HUMAN TOUCH

Back in the 1960s, social forecasters were predicting that salespeople would be made obsolete by the turn of the century through advances in computing and revolutionary marketing vehicles, such as direct mail and telemarketing. They could not have been more wrong. More people are selling today than ever before, and even professions that never considered using the "s" word in the past, such as banking, accounting, law, and medicine, find themselves soliciting business on a day-to-day basis. That's because consumers do not want to buy from a catalog, a piece of mail, or a voice on the telephone. They want to buy from a person who listens to them, understands their needs, and responds with appropriate products and services.

Offering your ideas

Many sales professionals think all they have to offer is their products and services. But it's not just what's in your bag that's important—it's what's in your head. When you present your customer with an idea that helps them do their job a bit better, teaches them something new, or addresses a personal issue, you are building value in your relationship that lets you leapfrog way ahead of your competitors.

Giving to receive

When a sales professional presents a customer with an idea that has no revenue attached to it, it's called an uncompensated idea. This is a great misnomer because surprising your customers with novel and unexpected thinking accumulates great value and brings long-term financial reward. If you're prepared to give, you will receive.

? ASK YOURSELF... ABOUT OFFERING NEW IDEAS

Before each client meeting, think of areas in which you could help the client by offering uncompensated ideas.

- Are they doing something we know they could do better with improved technology or software?
- What problems do they consistently raise—how hard is it for me to research them?
- Is there something in the client's nonworking life where I could offer an idea, for example, suggesting a venue for their child's party?
- Is there something about the client's facility that could be improved—a lack of signage, for example?
- Can I enhance the client's industry knowledge—by recommending a good seminar or training program?

Salespeople are reluctant to present uncompensated ideas for fear they will come across as inappropriate or embarrassing. So is it really worth taking the risk of crossing established boundaries? The answer is an emphatic "yes." When the customer sees you have put in effort to offer a new perspective they will know you value the relationship—even if they're not all that enthusiastic about the idea itself.

Adding value

The idea you offer up doesn't have to be related to business and it doesn't need to be Earth-shattering. However, it must add value. Don't present an idea just for the sake of doing so. Your customer doesn't know that you're about to offer an uncompensated idea, so before starting, get their permission. Let them know you have been thinking about their situation and you have an idea for them. Ask if they think it's appropriate for you to present it. Most customers will be intrigued. Next, express what you think their need is, present the idea, and explain its specific benefits. Be humble when you offer the idea and give credit to others whenever you can; there's nothing to be gained by trying to make the customer think you're smarter than they are.

TIP

TIME YOUR TIPS

Uncompensated ideas are best unveiled at the end of the meeting, not the beginning. They offer a great way to end any meeting on a high note.

CASE STUDY

Going the extra mile

An American training company was seeking bids for a new video system. It spoke to three potential suppliers, each of whom made good recommendations. There was little to choose among the three on price, quality, capabilities, and service agreements. While the company was in the decision-making process, the salesperson from one of the three suppliers emailed an article that appeared in *The Wall Street Journal* that day about one of the training company's clients. The email was accompanied by a short note: "I'm sure you saw this, but just in case…." Without other differentiators, the salesperson who took the extra step won the contract.

Asking for feedback

You have delivered your presentation. Your customers nodded enthusiastically throughout, so your recommendations must have been right on the mark. Or so you think. The only way to be sure and to move to the next stage of the selling process is to ask your client for feedback. It's time to hear from them.

TIP

GET YOUR TIMING RIGHT
You can ask for feedback at any time in your presentation. It's best to wait until you are finished so you don't get derailed, but if you suspect the customer has a strong concern, ask for feedback earlier.

Facing the music

Even seasoned salespeople will hesitate before asking the customer to respond to their recommendations. A lot of time went into getting to this point and the fear of rejection can be paralyzing. No matter how many times you tell yourself it's not you personally being rejected but your product or idea, it's hard not to take it that way. But don't make the mistake of delivering your recommendations, and then saying nothing and just waiting to hear from the customer. If you don't ask, you don't learn. Even if the answer may not be what you were hoping for, ask the question and move on.

Welcoming objections

When you ask for feedback, the response you get is usually an objection. You should accept now that people almost always object even when they are convinced they want to buy. There are complex reasons for this, and techniques for resolving objections will be explored in the next chapter. But for now, you should welcome the objection. If you had not given an opportunity for the objection to surface, it would have still existed in the customer's mind, and you would never have closed the deal. With the objection out in the open, you have a chance to work with the customer to resolve it.

Asking open questions

You will get better feedback if you ask the right questions. It's hard to rebound from a blunt "No" so use open-ended questions to elicit responses from the customer that you can work with. Your questions should be nonmanipulative and straightforward. Slippery sales patter like "Sounds pretty good doesn't it?" may antagonize the customer, so frame questions in a way that maintains the high level of dialogue that got you to this point.

"What do you think about our recommendation?"

"I've been talking for a while; now I'd love to hear from you."

"I would appreciate some feedback."

"I'd love to hear your reaction."

"So, what are your thoughts?"

"How does that sound?"

"Any questions?"

Chapter 4

Resolving objections and closing the sale

Resolving objections is often the most challenging part of the sales process—it can be uncomfortable and unpredictable. But understanding the situation and practicing your responses will help you perform well when you encounter resistance.

Understanding objections

Up to this point in the needs-driven selling model, your role has been that of facilitator and adviser. Now, when you start to encounter objections from the client, the role can feel a lot more like selling. However, there's no reason to freeze and miss the opportunity.

Making buying decisions

Most people object to a selling proposal even though they are interested in buying. It's human nature. The lesson to learn is that not all objections are as bad as they first appear, and most can be resolved.

So why do buyers object when they're ready to buy? Most are simply looking for reassurance from the salesperson. They want to feel like they are making good, thoughtful, reasonable decisions, and they don't want to think they are being hasty or foolish. They know they will start questioning themselves soon after they make the purchase.

You may have heard some of the terms associated with this phenomenon, such as buyer's remorse and cognitive dissonance*. When you make a decision to buy, especially when spending a lot of money, you may experience a sense of disequilibrium. Part of you feels good about the purchase, but part isn't so sure. It's not a comfortable feeling. Professional buyers are also subject to these feelings, so to protect themselves and feel like they are doing the right thing, they object—even when they may be ready to buy.

*Cognitive dissonance— a feeling of tension that arises when you keep two conflicting thoughts in mind simultaneously.

Reacting to resistance

Most salespeople react in one of three ways when faced with objections—becoming defensive, aggressive, or simply giving up. Not one of these is constructive, and not one is likely to help you close the deal. To keep from falling into one of these traps, do what you do best—problem solve with the customer.

The three common responses to resistance

BECOMING AGGRESSIVE
This suggests you must convince the customer you're right and, by implication, they are wrong. This doesn't encourage discussion.

GETTING DEFENSIVE
This sends out the message that the process is more about you than the client.

BECOMING PASSIVE
Giving up is worst of all. For all you know there may be considerable interest.

TIP

GET EXPERT HELP
Use all your resources when you encounter difficult objections. Consult with your colleagues, and invite experts to the presentation if you need support in specific areas.

Approaching conflict

Dealing with customers' objections is less daunting when you stick to a process derived from proven conflict-management techniques. This helps you focus on the objective, maintain your professionalism, and curbs your tendency to react too quickly.

Before introducing the objection-resolution model, there are two assumptions you need to accept. First, many, if not most, objections are unfulfilled needs. Needs are motivational in nature and when you don't meet them to the customer's satisfaction, they usually appear later as objections. Put another way, if you don't discover all the needs, you risk being blindsided later by an objection.

The second assumption, which may seem counterintuitive, is that most objections indicate interest at some level. Indifference and apathy are the reactions you want to see least in response to your recommendations. When the client complains about something, at least they care about the outcome. Taking the customer's objection as a good sign will encourage you to work to resolve it. It's a healthy way to approach conflict.

You don't have to accept these assumptions at face value, but work with them and decide later whether or not you agree.

IN FOCUS...
JUSTIFYING DECISIONS

People's desire to resolve the cognitive dissonance that accompanies buying decisions is illuminated by an observation from the advertising industry. A person is more likely to read an ad for a major purchase, such as an automobile, after they have bought the product than before the purchase. Reading the ad reinforces the correctness of the decision made in the buyer's mind.

Introducing the process

When you encounter resistance, start by acknowledging what the customer has said without responding to it with offense or defense. Next, ask questions to learn the totality of the objection. Make sure you have heard and understood the entire issue. Review your understanding with the customer of what is troubling them. Sometimes, you will simply need to paraphrase the objection in order to clarify it. At other times, you will have to reframe the objection and transform it into a need you can address. Next, address the concern as effectively as you can in order to resolve it. If the customer accepts your response, you should determine if there are other concerns. If there are, repeat the process. If there are none, close the sale.

Resolving objections is a linear process, similar in many ways to the needs-driven selling model as a whole. As with any other linear process, you don't have to use every step to succeed, but having a well-defined process to which to refer will help you deal with what most people find to be the hardest component of the sales process.

TIP

STEER TOWARD A SOLUTION

Think of yourself as a facilitator when you resolve objections. It's your job to lead the way as you navigate toward resolution.

ASK YOURSELF... ABOUT YOUR BUYING BEHAVIOR

You can learn about your client's attitudes by reviewing how you react when you make a significant purchase.

- What reasons do I come up with to delay or prevent a buying decision?
- How much is my behavior shaped by the salesperson?
- Do I object because it helps me feel more confident about my purchase?
- Do I object because I want to test the salesperson?
- How do I react to an aggressive sell?

Collecting the data

The first two steps in the objection resolution process are acknowledging the client's objections and asking them to elaborate on their concerns. Posing the right questions helps you collect the critical data you need to understand and deal with the customer's objection.

TRANSFER YOUR SKILLS

Acknowledging is more than just a tool for use in the selling process—it is a life skill. Use it with your significant other, colleagues, children, even strangers. When you acknowledge how someone may feel, good things usually follow.

Acknowledging objections

Your goal at this point is to encourage your customer to open up about their objections. To begin this process, you should acknowledge their concerns. This doesn't mean agreeing with their objections (which would suggest a lack of conviction on your part) or implying that you disagree (which would set the scene for confrontation). Instead, simply recognize their right to object, demonstrate empathy, and show you are amenable to discussing the situation. They will see you are willing, and hopefully able, to solve the problem.

A good technique for acknowledging objections is to reflect the customer's own language in your response. Aim to paraphrase their objection, without being patronizing. For example, if they bring up the objection that your product is far too expensive, you could reply "I recognize that expense is a big concern for you."

Below are some examples of the types of phrases you can use to acknowledge objections:
- "I can see why…"
- "I appreciate that investing in our system may seem daunting…"
- "That's a fair question…"
- "I think I understand why you might feel that way based on what you've heard so far…"
- "I appreciate your candor…"
- "I guess I wasn't as clear as I wanted to be…"

Questioning the client

The customer's stated objections are often just the tip of the iceberg. They may not be expressing all their concerns, or may be masking their true objections. To get to the bottom of their concerns, you need to start asking questions. Keep these questions crisp, open-ended, and void of content so you don't "lead the witness." For example, if a client voices a general objection, don't ask, "Is it the price?" This will succeed only in making them suspicious of price—you will have given them another reason not to buy! Instead, try something like: "Could you be more specific?" This will encourage the customer to elaborate without giving them new reasons to object. Similar question phrasings include:
- "Would you please elaborate?"
- "Can you say a little more about that?"
- "Why is that?"
- "I'm not sure I understand. Could you clarify?"

TIP

BE RESTRAINED

Don't go too far in expressing your desire to work with a prospect—it can work against you.

ASKING QUESTIONS

⬆ FAST TRACK	⚫ OFF TRACK
Being objective	Appearing judgmental
Staying in control	Displaying emotion
Asking open-ended questions	Asking leading questions or patronizing the client
Being straightforward	Being perceived as manipulative
Using appreciative phrases	Being an interrogator

Being sensitive

When you deal with the client's objections, don't forget you are in conflict-resolution mode and sensitivity on your part is not only desirable but critical. The questioning process must not seem like an interrogation—it needs to be a comfortable experience for the customer so he or she will explain their concerns and continue the dialogue. As with much of what has an impact on the sales process, it's how you do it that matters most.

Accepting objections

Of course, there are times when you should agree with what the customer is saying, but without closing off the conversation. For example, if your product is more expensive than the competition's and you are unable to shift on price, your reply could be: "Yes, it is expensive, but I hope you think it's worth discussing its cost in respect of what it can do for you."

 IN FOCUS...
CROSSING THE LINE

Almost any positive behavior can become a negative one when used in excess. Curiosity is great until it becomes nosiness. You should be assertive but not aggressive. By all means be pleasant but avoid being obsequious. Be empathetic and customer-focused, but don't appear patronizing. Take a position, but don't become dogmatic. And, of course, be tenacious, just don't get stubborn. These distinctions become particularly important when resolving conflict, but if you trust your instincts and build on them with experience, you'll be right a lot more than you'll be wrong.

BE POSITIVE
Let your customer know you appreciate their insights by interspersing your questions with appreciative phrases such as: "Thank you" and "That's very helpful."

BE DIRECT
Clearly signal your intentions using phrases such as: "I'd like to ask another question or two in order to…" to make the climate more conducive to problem solving.

Encouraging the customer to open up

INTRODUCE YOUR QUESTIONS
Give reasons why you need the information to help diffuse suspicion and put the customer at ease. If your customer raises the objection that your solution is complicated, respond with: "Yes, it is complex—but it's also very manageable. Can we discuss this further…?"

MIRROR THE CLIENT
If the client becomes obstructive and puts you on the wrong foot, try mirroring his or her objections. For example, counter "Your suggestion is ridiculous" with "Why do you think this seems ridiculous?" Do this in a nonjudgmental way that conveys your real curiosity about the answer.

BE SILENT
Sometimes, and especially when a client reacts in an inappropriately strong manner, being silent is the best option. Silence can defuse the situation and give the client time to realize that his or her behavior is not contributing to a resolution.

Reframing objections

By this time, you have heard the customer's objections to your proposal. Most—but not all—objections you will hear from clients are really disguised, unfulfilled needs. So the next step of the selling process is reframing* the objections as needs.

Translating into needs

*__Reframing__—the art of turning a negative into a positive, changing the apparently unresolvable into the possible.

Objections from customers are barriers to progress, whereas needs are aspirational, so it follows that turning objections into needs makes them easier to discuss and resolve. These examples illustrate how objections in fact mask needs:

• A client complains about the high complexity of your proposal: what he may need is a clearer explanation of how it works pitched at his own level.
• A client recounts a bad experience of a purchase similar to the one you are proposing: what she may need is reassurance that it won't happen again.
• A client laments the difficulty of changing their in-house systems: he may need to understand that you can help to facilitate the process.

CUSTOMER
We've used our existing suppliers for eight years

SALESPERSON
Naturally, you need to know the work is secure in our hands

CUSTOMER
It's not workable—you're based too far from our offices

SALESPERSON
There's a need to identify tasks that demand close collaboration

You can reframe almost any objection into an invitational question that asks how something can be done as opposed to why it can't. An objection like "My manager will never go for this" becomes "It appears to me there's a need to establish a rock-solid business case for this purchase."

When you reframe a client's objection you are changing the tone of what they said, and you should refrain from putting words into their mouth. Note the use of "it appears to me" in the example above.

TIP

KEEP TRYING

Don't worry if the way you reframe the objection is off target. Ask the customer to correct you and keep trying until you get it right.

Setting objectives

When you reframe the concern as a need, make sure it is a need you are able to address. For example, don't say something like "It seems like you need to get a lower price" if you can't move on price. Instead, try "As I understand, you need to see more clearly the cost/value equation here."

After you have reframed the objection, confirm with the customer that they agree with your interpretation. You have now converted their objection into a new objective—with the client's agreement you can now move toward meeting the objective and edge closer to closing the deal.

CASE STUDY

Reframing for success

Reframing is not restricted to selling situations. A multibillion dollar company was in the process of selecting a new CEO. During the interviews, one of the leading candidates was challenged by the chairman. The candidate had a reputation for taking risks, and the chairman expressed his worries about his judgment in financial decisions. The candidate's reframe went something like this: "My impression is that you're concerned about my reputation for trying new things and need to feel comfortable that when it comes to financial decisions I will demonstrate the fiduciary responsibility the job demands. Is that correct?" He gave a great response and two days later he got the job.

Discussing price

Customers will always complain about price. Indeed, price resistance is the most common objection salespeople will encounter, and it can be the hardest to resolve. However, as with other types of objection, understanding why the customer is objecting and turning that objection into a need can be an effective way of managing the resistance.

TIP

BE CLEAR ABOUT THE VALUE
Don't confuse price with value. People are always willing to pay more if they understand the value they are getting for their money.

Understanding price resistance

Everyone wants to find a good deal and feel that they are getting a competitive price. However, objections about price are sometimes used as a convenient and acceptable reason to object, but can be a smokescreen to mask other issues. In these situations, it is important that you question your customer to determine what the underlying issue really is. At other times, however, the objection truly is all about price. In instances where the buyer is making his or her decision on price alone, there may be little leeway for negotiation, and you may choose to walk away from the relationship.

Preempting the objection

If you have undergone a thorough needs determination, when you make a recommendation your customer should not be surprised or shocked about the price. Needs determination should include a discussion of what the customer is currently paying or expects to pay. Questioning the customer about their budget or pricing guidelines will help you recommend a price close to what is expected. If the customer won't answer your questions, give them a "sense of" cost: "Just so you know, a program like this typically costs $150. How does that sound?" You will quickly find out whether this is a long way from what they expect to pay.

Resolving price objections

The objection-resolution process is your best tool in dealing with price objections. First, acknowledge the objection as you would any other, for example: "I know you are trying to keep costs down." Next, get the customer talking. Ask questions, and find out about any other offers they have had from your competitors—how do they compare to yours? Are the deals comparable with yours in terms of the value delivered? Learn as much as you can regarding how far off you are in price from other offers.

When resolving price objections, reframing the objection is critical. Do everything you can to turn your customer's objection into need, using phrases such as: "So if I understand you correctly, you need to know what you will get for the additional 10 percent," "My understanding is that you need to understand why we charge a bit more than X and why it's still in your interest to buy from us…"; or "It appears to me you need to feel comfortable with your decision to pay us more than some of our competitors…"

If the customer agrees with your reframe, go ahead and address the need. Give it your best shot, and see if they will accept your point of view. You will be surprised how an objection often turns out to be less significant than it originally appeared to be.

TIP

CHOOSE YOUR QUESTIONS CAREFULLY

Getting a customer to elaborate about price or cost issues is a delicate matter. Be sensitive in your approach, using questions such as "How far off are we?" or "Can you tell us a bit more?"

IN FOCUS... LOWERING YOUR PRICE

The last thing you should do is lower your price without taking something off the table. If you provide a quote and a customer objects and you then subsequently drop your price, the message is clear—you were charging too much originally. This sentiment can have serious negative impact on further business and how you are perceived. If you do have to lower your price (which happens), let the customer know what you have to remove or reduce from the original proposal. As a last resort, let them know you are lowering the price to earn your way in, but that the original price was fair and this is a short-term offer you will not repeat.

Responding to objections

Once you have reformulated your customer's objection into a need, it's time to respond. Usually, this is straightforward—the answers lie in what you have already proposed and in knowledge you already have—but sometimes you will need to be creative to lead your client to a solution.

Playing to your strengths

Before you can move to the final stage of the selling process—closing—you need to deal definitively with the customer's objections (or unfulfilled needs, as we know them) by using all means at your disposal (see opposite). If you still cannot resolve the objections, you need to revert to problem-solving mode. If you still draw a blank, call time out and ask to come back in a day or two with fresh ideas to move forward. Your customer will respect you for it in the long run.

TIP

BE RELAXED
Remember that some questions customers ask are not objections but simply straightforward questions. Just because someone asks you about inventory issues doesn't necessarily mean they are worried about them.

Mopping up the concerns

Your final act in the objection-resolution process is to learn if there are other objections. This may sound like opening Pandora's Box, but it's critical. If other objections do exist, you need to learn about them because if you fail to uncover them now, they will certainly spoil the deal later. So ask the question. Keep your inquiry neutral and use expressions such as: "Is there anything else we need to discuss?" Try to stay away from negative language and terms such as "objections" or "issues" or "concerns." If you use words like these, you can give the customer the impression you know something they don't. Keep it simple. If objections remain, reloop and repeat the process until you have removed all the obstacles that stand in the way of closing.

CREATE CONFIDENCE IN YOUR SOLUTION
Review similar problems you have solved for other clients.

Closing in on closing

HIGHLIGHT THE SPECIFIC BENEFITS
Repeat or rephrase a benefit the client has forgotten or did not fully appreciate during the earlier presentation phase.

REVIEW THE FEATURES AND BENEFITS
Go back over these trusted selling tools.

SELL YOURSELF
Make your customer feel confident in your ability. Explain why you're so well placed to address their concerns about service, quality, or specification.

SELL YOUR COLLEAGUES
Make sure the customer knows you're part of a dedicated and responsive team.

GET CREATIVE
Generate ideas together with your client to modify the strategy. Use inclusive language when describing how to overcome objections: "*we* have to figure out why..." or "*our* priority now is to..."

SELL YOUR COMPANY
Talk about your company's history, successes, and commitment to excellence.

Closing the sale

Over the years, salespeople's ingenuity has given life to scores of "sure-fire" closing techniques. Going by names such as the Puppy-dog Close, the Distraction Close, and the Treat Close, some are just gimmicky, while others border on the manipulative. Their faults lie in the fact that they all see closing as a special technique, rather than the natural outcome of a problem-solving dialogue with the client.

TIP

BE GRACIOUS
Always thank the customer for their business—it is the classy thing to do.

Approaching the close

You have built the relationship, determined the needs, made great recommendations, and resolved the customer's objections. It's time to close—to ask for the business. So why do so many sales professionals find this step so difficult? The answer is simple—it is that fear of rejection rearing its ugly head once again. This fear pushes many experienced salespeople toward canned "closes," like the Specific Terms Close, where the idea is to present the customer with a prearranged buying scenario, and then ask them to agree to it. For example, "We can deliver 10 units on May 12th for $1,000. Is that OK?" Of course, on occasion, this approach—and others in a similar vein—may bring about a sale, but often the customer will think you are being rude and presumptuous. It's canned selling at its lowest.

Assuming the best

To close a deal you shouldn't need to rely on corny closing tactics. You need simply to demonstrate the same credibility, integrity, and degree of interaction with the customer you showed throughout the selling process. Don't change the basis of your hard-won relationship at this point.

Assume that if the customer does not have a reason not to buy, he or she is ready to buy. This is called the Assumptive Close. In this Assumptive Close, the dialogue with the customer is direct, and goes something like this:

SALESPERSON: "Anything else we need to discuss?"

CUSTOMER: "No, not that I can think of."

SALESPERSON: "So everything seems OK?"

CUSTOMER: "Yes. I believe so."

The point is clear even though the words you choose may vary—you ask the customer if there are other concerns. If they say no, you double check. If everything seems OK, just ask for the business.

SALESPERSON: **"Great! Then how do we get started?"**

Asking and getting

If you've done your job well up to this point, the customer will know you have something valuable to offer and will want to buy from you; moreover they'll want you to ask for their business. If you don't, you're expecting the customer to do your job. It seems obvious, but if you don't ask for the business, you're much less likely to get it.

Planning for completion

Once there has been a commitment to buy, close the sale by beginning to pin down the specifics. A good way to cover all the key variables is to answer the "four Ws"—who will do what by when with help from whom? When you have the answers to these questions, you are ready to execute.

If you don't close the deal—and of course you won't always—it is vital to keep the momentum of the selling process going. Set objectives for resolving issues and be clear about what has to be done before the next meeting. Experienced salespeople will tell you the only time you fail in a sales call is when you don't get a next step.

Consolidating the close

Everyone needs reassurance after making a large purchase—to silence the nagging voice asking if they did the right thing (discussed earlier in this chapter). With this in mind, it is important to make sure you are highly visible to the customer after you have closed the deal. Some salespeople say that "the real selling starts after you get the business," and it's hard to argue with that sentiment. With hard work, anyone can get the first order; it's the people who get the second, third, and fourth who are most successful. Whatever you do, don't fall into the stereotypical image of a "love 'em and leave 'em" salesperson. If you do, your relationship will be a short one. Guaranteed!

To be successful repeatedly, you need to acknowledge the transfer of power that occurs when the deal is closed. When a customer is a prospect, they hold all the cards, but once they commit to the deal, they lose some of that power because they are dependent on you to deliver. It's uncomfortable for them, and it is a good reason for you to show humility after closing the deal. It's not the time to whoop and punch the air.

TIP

JUST ASK

Ask for the business, even if it feels uncomfortable. Research has revealed that customers rank asking for their business as the sixth most important reason for doing the deal.

Collecting for success

There is a distasteful acronym out there in the world of selling—ABC, Always Be Closing—which reflects the strong emphasis placed on closing by many sales managers. Of course, closing is important, but it shouldn't be viewed as an isolated goal. Transform this unhealthy acronym into an ABC that will help you—Always Be Collecting. Only when you consistently question, understand, and resolve issues together with your customer will you be on the road to success.

CASE STUDY

Using a "closer"

A young salesman had called on the same client twice a month for two years. Sensing he was close to his first order, he brought his boss with him. The junior salesman reviewed price agreements, credit terms, and product specifications with the client. He kept asking the customer if everything was approved, whether they were satisfied, and if there were any other questions. All the answers were positive, but the salesman just couldn't pull the trigger. Finally, the manager lost patience and blurted out

"Well then, how about an order?" The customer's response was "What took you so long to ask?"

The customer was obviously ready to buy and the young salesman's reluctance to close was only raising suspicions in the client's mind. If the manager hadn't stepped in, the sale could have been lost.

However, using a more senior person as a "closer" is a poor selling model. The salesperson should feel adequately equipped, trained, and empowered to ask for the business.

Moving beyond the close

After you have closed, you earn yet another great opportunity to differentiate yourself from the competition. Following through goes beyond just following up on your promises—doing what you said you would do professionally and on time. Following through means exceeding what's expected of you and so sending the clear message to your customers that you are consistently thinking about them.

Following up

Follow-up is doing whatever you committed to do at the end of the sales meeting with your customer. It is a process you initiate to ensure objectives are accomplished and commitments are fulfilled. It is your responsibility to make sure all of your organization's resources are doing what is needed to move the relationship to the next level. Will the samples be there on time? Is everyone aware of and able to meet the agreed upon delivery dates? Is the team committed to participate in the next meeting?

Every single sales call you make—from a brief catch-up meeting to a formal presentation—deserves a follow-up letter. This can be a letter, an email, or even a handwritten note—whatever suits both your style and the occasion—but must follow every call.

 IN FOCUS... TRACKING CONTACT

Time speeds by. It's not hard for 90 days to pass before you realize you haven't made any contact with a customer. "Out of sight, out of mind" may be a cliché, but it's true. And if you haven't been in touch with a client, it's a safe bet your competitor has. To prevent long silences from developing, track how often you make contact with your customers. Use a spreadsheet, datebook, or whatever suits your style to record every face-to-face meeting, as well as phone calls, letters, and emails.

The letter should thank the customer for their time, review what was discussed, and define the next steps. It can also serve as a reminder of who committed to do what by when.

Following through

When you follow through, you do more than you need to. Here are some ways you can surprise your customers with your level of commitment:
• Regularly check how things are progressing internally, and communicate effectively to everybody involved on a day-to-day basis.
• Send your customers a list of follow-up activities and deliverables, including dates; make sure you meet them consistently.
• Let your customer know well in advance if for some reason you can't meet a deliverable.
• Send emails updating your customers without requesting a response. This instills confidence that you have their interests in mind all the time.

MAKING THE MARK

FAST TRACK	OFF TRACK
Promising and delivering	Overpromising and underdelivering
Putting it in writing	Assuming the customer understands
Being visible	Being a nuisance
Being consistently professional	Forgetting details
Showing interest in doing business	Appearing desperate or overanxious

NEGOTIATING

Contents

Introduction

Negotiation is challenging, complex, and exciting, and requires a mixture of knowledge, skills, experience, and intuition. Each negotiation is unique and there is no single technique for improving your success. Thus, to be a successful negotiator, you should use a mixture of moves and countermoves, driven by the nature of the specific negotiating situation. This book describes various practices and techniques that can help make you a more successful negotiator in every situation you face.

Negotiating distills negotiation theory and practice to give you practical advice on how to become a successful negotiator. It addresses questions such as: "Should I make the first offer?"; "How should I present and respond to offers?"; "How can I obtain concessions from my counterpart?"; and "How can I make concessions effectively?" It helps you understand and put into practice ways to analyze your and your counterpart's power, and to increase your negotiating power by building winning coalitions.

However, negotiating successfully goes beyond mastering tactics and strategies. It is also about having the right attitude and mindset, such as being diligent in your preparation and planning; being resilient in the face of multiple challenges; being creative by inventing mutually beneficial options; and being ready to walk away from poor deals. By mastering these negotiating tactics and strategies, and by developing the right attitude and mindset, you will achieve superior results.

Chapter 1

Preparing to negotiate

Negotiation is a skill you can learn and develop through practice and experience. By framing the process correctly and searching in advance for creative options, you will be able to find solutions that satisfy the interests of all parties.

Becoming a negotiator

Many people shy away from negotiation because they think it implies conflict. In fact, negotiation is what you make it. When undertaken with confidence and understanding, negotiation is a creative interpersonal process in which two parties collaborate to achieve superior results.

Seeing the benefits

When you become skilled in negotiation, you can create real value for your organization. Negotiation allows you, for example, to secure cost-effective and reliable flows of supplies, enhance the financial value of mergers and acquisitions, settle potentially damaging disputes with union leaders or government officials, or resolve internal conflict constructively. Negotiation is increasingly recognized as a core competency. Many companies develop their own methodologies and offer training and mentoring programs for negotiators.

Understanding the basics

Good negotiators are made rather than born. Although some may be naturally gifted and intuitive (possessing, for example, the ability to empathize with others), most have developed their principles and tactics over time and recognize that negotiating is a largely rational process.

To be a successful negotiator, you have to feel psychologically comfortable in the negotiation situation. This means being able to tolerate uncertainty, deal with unexpected behavior, take measured risks, and make decisions based on incomplete information. You need to think about solving problems and creating opportunities rather than winning or losing. If you are confrontational, you are likely to have a fight on your hands. And if you "win" there will necessarily be a loser, with whom you may have to work in the months to come.

TIP

LEARN YOUR ART

Developing the skills needed to be a successful negotiator can take time, so be patient. Try to learn from every negotiation you undertake, both for your organization and in your life outside work.

BUILDING A FOUNDATION

FAST TRACK	OFF TRACK
Keeping an open mind about learning new techniques	Believing that negotiating is an innate ability
Treating negotiation skills as a mixture of rationality and intuition	Negotiating from a fixed viewpoint
Developing trust slowly	Appearing too eager
Expressing empathy while negotiating assertively	Behaving assertively without expressing empathy
Having a strategy and sticking to it	Chasing haphazard opportunities

Understanding negotiation dilemmas

The negotiating task is very complex because it embodies a number of fundamental dilemmas. To be successful in your negotiations, you need to understand the difference between the true dilemmas you need to address, and the many myths that surround negotiating.

Identifying true dilemmas

Over time, a number of myths have evolved about the nature of negotiations. Many negotiators continue to hold to them, failing to recognize the difference between these myths and the real dilemmas they face. For example, it is a popular misconception that a negotiator must either be consistently "tough" or consistently "soft" if they are to be successful. In reality, effective negotiators do not need to choose between these approaches, but must be flexible and use a repertoire of styles.

THE STRATEGY OR OPPORTUNITY DILEMMA
Unexpected opportunities sometimes arise in negotiation. It can be tempting to divert from your well-planned strategy, but be aware that this may distract you from achieving your objectives.

Many also believe negotiation is largely an intuitive act, rather than a rational process. It is true that an effective negotiator will use their intuition to a certain extent (to know the right moment to make a concession or present an offer, for example). However, most of the negotiating task requires systematic processes such as masterful due diligence, identifying interests, and setting clear objectives.

Skilled negotiators are able to recognize the myths and focus their energy on the true negotiation dilemmas, balancing their approach and making the difficult decisions needed to achieve the most successful outcomes in their negotiations.

THE HONESTY DILEMMA

How much should you tell the other party? If you tell them everything, they may exploit the information and take advantage of you, so you need to strike a balance between honesty and transparency.

THE TRUST DILEMMA

Trust is needed for a negotiation to move forward, but if you trust the other party completely, you put yourself at risk of being taken advantage of. Invest in building trust, albeit with measured caution.

The five negotiation dilemmas

THE EMPATHY DILEMMA

If you develop empathy with the other party, it may stop you from acting assertively and negotiating for your interests. Try to do both well—maintain good relationships, but protect your interests, too.

THE COMPETE OR COOPERATE DILEMMA

You must compete for the benefits on the table, but also cooperate to create them with the other party. You therefore need to be skilled at both, to be able to create and then claim value.

Being prepared

Your success in a negotiation depends largely on the quality of your preparation. Start by thinking through your position and your objectives. Having clear goals will protect you from making too many concessions and motivate you to perform better. Objectives should be specific, quantifiable, and measurable. Only then can they be used as benchmarks to measure your progress during the negotiation process.

TIP

VALUE THE ISSUES
Draw up a list of potential negotiating points, starting with the most critical. Give each issue a value, and estimate the value your counterpart is likely to place on it.

Setting the limits

You should always go to the negotiating table with clear answers to the following questions: Why do you want to negotiate the deal? How will this deal create value for you? What are your "deal breakers"? What must you have from the deal; what would you like; and what are you willing to give away? There may be alternative outcomes you can accept—what are they?

Knowing your objectives

Set your objectives high but not outrageously so. It is tempting to censor your aspirations, setting them too low to protect yourself from the prospect of failure, but in doing so, you will almost certainly achieve less than was possible. If you fail to set clear objectives, there is also a danger you could get trapped in an "escalation of commitment"—an irrational urge to "win" the negotiation at any cost.

Escalation of commitment is a very real hazard in negotiation, and happens when you refuse to give up your pursuit of a negative course of action when the wiser choice would be to cut your losses and move on. Always set a limit for how far you are prepared to go and prepare an exit strategy (a means of walking away from the deal).

IN FOCUS... AVOIDING ESCALATION OF COMMITMENT

It can be easy to fall into the trap of competing with the other party at all costs, to make sure that you get that "win." For example, in the late 1980s, Robert Campeau, a Canadian businessman, made a hostile bid to acquire Federated Department Stores (FDS). Macy's, a competitor of FDS, was also interested and a bidding war began between Campeau and Macy's.

Determined to win, Campeau kept increasing his already high bids to a point where he offered to pay an additional $500 million. Campeau won the competition, but two years later he declared bankruptcy. This is a classic case of escalation of commitment, and a lesson for all negotiators in keeping a sense of perspective in their negotiations.

Looking across the table

A negotiator was once asked if he could formulate a proposal that took into consideration both his and his counterpart's interests. He was puzzled. He asked: "Why should I care about the other party's interests? His interests are his problem." Such an attitude of blinkered self-interest characterizes the unprepared negotiator. In order to succeed, you not only need to understand yourself and your interests, but also the other negotiating party, and the situation as a whole. Ask yourself the following questions when preparing for a negotiation:

• Who will come to the table? Research their personality, and their history of negotiation. Have they previously been successful or unsuccessful, and what approaches did they use?
• What can you find out about their negotiating style, life history, hobbies, and interests?
• If you have more than one counterpart, do they share the same backgrounds and functional area and are they likely to be united in their desired outcome?
• Are they authorized to make binding decisions? If not, who are the "players" behind the scenes who will make the final decision?

TIP

DO THE RESEARCH
Information is power. Find out as much as you can about your counterpart before you sit down to negotiate.

Understanding your counterpart

It is important to understand the issues and interests of the other party before you start the negotiations. Negotiators come to the table because they each need something from the other, so you must identify your counterpart's key issues and interests. How important is each one? Which are the deal breakers and which may they be willing to concede?

Try to assess whether it is you or your counterpart who holds the power. What are your counterpart's strengths and weaknesses? What is their level of information and expertise? How badly do they want to make a deal with you? Do they have other attractive options? Can they walk away from the table and exercise a BATNA*? Are they pressed for time? If you know the other side has a tight deadline that you are able to meet, you may be able to negotiate a better price. Similarly, if you know your counterpart has recently expanded production capacity, you may be able to gain better terms for larger volumes of orders.

***BATNA**—acronym of Best Alternative To a Negotiated Agreement. This term is used by negotiators to describe the course of action you (or your counterpart) will take if negotiations break down.*

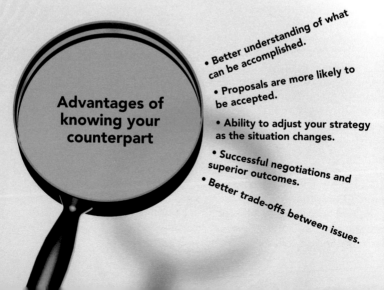

Advantages of knowing your counterpart

- Better understanding of what can be accomplished.
- Proposals are more likely to be accepted.
- Ability to adjust your strategy as the situation changes.
- Successful negotiations and superior outcomes.
- Better trade-offs between issues.

Thinking strategically

Much of what occurs in the negotiating room is, in fact, determined by what happens outside the negotiating room. This requires you to think strategically about your situation in relation to the situation of your negotiating counterpart. For example, in some negotiations, you and the other party may be representing others. Make sure you are very clear about the identity of your constituency, and that of your counterpart. What are their expectations and can you influence them?

If there are several negotiating parties, analyze all of them and begin to think in terms of coalitions. With whom and how can you build a winning coalition and how can you block a threatening coalition?

TIP

CONSIDER THE TIMESCALE

Shape your negotiating strategy with respect to the timescale. You can be more blunt in a short, once-only negotiation than in a long negotiation that is part of an ongoing relationship.

Tailoring your strategy

Make sure your negotiating strategy and behavior reflect the other party's situation and approach. For example, in many negotiations, the other party is free to leave or join the negotiating table as they wish. In some cases, however, the parties are bonded together over the long term and cannot simply walk away, and your strategy should reflect this.

Some negotiators prefer to negotiate away from the public eye, while others insist on keeping all stakeholders and the public informed. Consider which mode is more advantageous to you, taking into account the sensitivity of the issues, the history between the parties, and the legal and governance systems of each party.

Some negotiation counterparts observe formal protocols in negotiations, while others are freer in what can and cannot be said. Be absolutely sure to do your research thoroughly when negotiating internationally to learn the formalities expected of you.

Designing the structure

Before producing a blueprint for a building, an architect first studies the functionality of the structure—the purpose it will serve. When you are planning a negotiation, you need to think like an architect and devise a structure and a process that will best fit the purpose of the negotiation.

TIP

CREATING THE RIGHT TEAM

In team negotiations, carefully consider the size and composition of your team so you include all necessary skills and represent all key constituents.

Structuring your approach

Every successful negotiation starts with a clear structure: defined roles; agreed upon rules; a set agenda; and a schedule for action. A framework for the negotiation will most likely be suggested by each of the participants. It is then subject to negotiation and joint re-creation so all parties are satisfied it reflects their concerns. Consult with the party in negotiation before you negotiate to agree to all procedures you will use. If you cannot agree on the procedures, it may be better to postpone or abandon the negotiations altogether.

Making a framework

Your agreed upon framework needs to be sufficiently flexible to accommodate changes in circumstance, but should at very least cover the following:

• **Basic ground rules** These need to be agreed to with your counterpart. For example, is it acceptable to change negotiators midstream? Are observers allowed? Is the meeting open or closed? How should people be addressed and how should priority of speech be given? What will be the course of action if you cannot reach agreement? All parties should agree to listen respectfully to one another, attempt to understand the positions of others, and refrain from legal proceedings for the duration of the negotiation.

• **A clear agenda** This should include all the substantive issues and interests you and the opposition wish to negotiate. Clarify the level of importance of each issue and decide the order in which issues should be discussed. Some negotiators prefer to start with easy issues, others tackle everything at once.

• **An agreed upon venue** Chinese philosopher Sun Tzu's *Art of War* states that one should "lure the tiger from the mountain," that is, make your counterpart leave their comfortable environment. Ask yourself how the choice of venue will affect you and your team. At the very least, make sure you will have access to the necessary support (computers, secure phone lines, and advisers).

Managing processes

Once you have an agreed upon framework in place, you also need to structure the processes that will steer the negotiation through its various phases. There are three distinct processes—the negotiation process, the temporal process, and the psychosocial process—that come together in any negotiation. Each requires a different set of skills.

The negotiation process involves managing information and communications during the discussions, planning and replanning, coordinating efforts between negotiators, making moves and countermoves (all in real time), and making important decisions under conditions of uncertainty and time pressure.

Keeping time

The temporal process involves managing time and the way in which the negotiation moves from one stage to the next by appropriately pacing the speed of each stage and synchronizing the actions of the negotiators. Many negotiations (and sales presentations) stall because the negotiators labor points for too long and are unable or unwilling to move the process toward its closure phase.

Thinking straight

The psychosocial process requires a sound knowledge of human behavior and an understanding that people will take on "roles" during negotiations. You need to be able to overcome barriers to rational negotiation and avoid psychological traps, such as the illusion of optimism, a sense of superiority, and overconfidence. Other hazards include a reluctance to reverse a decision that produces poor results or intense conflict, and competition between negotiators on the same team.

Playing by the rules

The purpose of processes and structures is not to constrain the progress of the negotiation, but to give you tools to resolve challenges or impasses. Having clear rules will allow you to:
• Move from multiparty negotiations to one-on-one negotiations.
• Change the level of negotiation, upward or downward.
• Replace negotiators who are self-serving or too rigid.
• Expedite the process by issuing a deadline.
• Change the venue or schedule.
• Conduct some of the negotiations behind the scenes by introducing a back channel.

Avoiding common mistakes

Never underestimate the risks associated with poor preparation. When you fail to plan, you plan to fail. The most common errors in forward planning include:

RELYING ON SECONDARY INFORMATION
Always seek out reliable sources of primary information. By all means read industry report analyses, reports of management projections, and corporate annual reports, but consider that these reports may sometimes be inaccurate or biased.

AVAILABILITY BIAS
It is easy to find information that is widely available. Make an effort to uncover information that is not so easy to obtain.

CONFIRMATORY BIAS
Do not filter out important information because it does not fit with your existing points of view and beliefs.

INFORMATION ASYMMETRY
Do you really know as much as you think? To be safe, you should assume by default that you know less than the other party.

OVERCONFIDENCE
If you underestimate your counterpart you will neglect to plan well. If you already think you know how a negotiation will end, you may exclude new sources of information and creative solutions.

UNDERESTIMATING RESOURCES
In any negotiation you must be able to present supporting facts, anticipate how the other side will respond to your arguments, and prepare counterarguments. Do not underestimate how long it can take to assemble such information, especially if you require input from experts and colleagues.

Chapter 2

Setting your style

There are many approaches to negotiation. Some negotiators advocate a hard-line, uncompromising style. Skilled negotiators know you are more likely to achieve a satisfactory outcome by taking the interests of the other party into account and trying to create win–win deals, develop mutual trust, and build relationships for the future.

Defining negotiation styles

Negotiators come to the negotiation table because they have needs they believe may be fulfilled through negotiations. In order to fulfill these needs, negotiators use different styles and engage in a variety of behaviors that they trust will help them get what they want.

*Value-claiming behavior— *competitive actions undertaken by a negotiator in an attempt to ensure a win–lose outcome in their favor. Such actions include making excessive demands or threats, concealing interests, and withholding information.*

Identifying different approaches

There are three styles of negotiation: distributive, integrative, and mixed motive. Negotiators who use the distributive style view negotiations as a competitive sport, a zero-sum game with a winner and a loser. Such negotiators compete fiercely for the distribution of the outcomes (the size of the pie) and engage in value-claiming behavior*. They dismiss the value of building relationships and trust as naive, tend to use threats to obtain concessions, and exaggerate the value of the small concessions they make. They also conceal their needs, do not share information, do not look for possible creative ideas, and even use deceptive tactics. In contrast to value-claiming negotiators, integrative negotiators believe the size of the pie is not fixed and can be expanded, and that the negotiation process is able to produce a win–win solution. The integrative style of negotiation is designed to integrate the needs of all the negotiators. Negotiators engage in value-creation behaviors. They invest in building relationships and nurturing trust, share information openly, and are cooperative, flexible, and creative.

TIP

TAILOR YOUR APPROACH

Utilize all of the negotiation styles—distributive, integrative, and mixed—where appropriate, depending on who you are negotiating with and what their negotiating style is.

Using mixed-motive tactics

The true nature of effective negotiations is often mixed, requiring both cooperative and competitive tactics. The rationale for this is that, through cooperation, negotiators create value; they put money on the table. Following this, once value has been created and the money is on the table, the parties have to split it among themselves. In order to secure the most profitable split, a negotiator has to switch from the cooperative mode to the competitive mode.

 IN FOCUS... RESPONSES TO DISTRIBUTIVE TACTICS

If the other party is using a distributive win–lose approach, a negotiator who favors the win–win style must protect their own interests. Some respond with the same hard tactics, meeting toughness with toughness. However, because the win–lose negotiation style is most likely to produce suboptimal outcomes, it is advisable to first try to influence the other party to move toward a more integrative style. Value claimants often think the other party is oblivious to their tactics, and so some negotiators inform the other party tactfully but firmly that they know what they are doing and that it doesn't contribute to productive negotiations. If all approaches to dealing with value-claiming tactics fail, however, and if they do not require the deal, many negotiators will simply leave the table.

Defining interest-based negotiation

Negotiators often make the mistake of turning the negotiation process into a contest of positions. Some are hard bargainers, thinking of the other party as an adversary; others take a soft approach, considering the other person to be a friend and making concessions easily. Instead of utilizing hard or soft bargaining tools, effective negotiators tend to focus on the interests of both parties.

Focusing on interests

In interest-based negotiation, the negotiators come to the table with a clear understanding of what they want and why they want it, but also with an understanding that the other party has its own set of needs to fulfill. Knowing that both parties' needs can be satisfied in multiple ways allows for the negotiation process to be more about constructive problem-solving—that is, collaborating to find out what they can do together in order to achieve their respective interests.

Focusing on interests involves concentrating on the "why" instead of the "what." People always have a reason for wanting something. For example, imagine you and your friend are arguing over who should have the last orange in the fruit bowl. Your friend may want the orange because she wants to make juice, while you may want it because you need the zest to make cake. If, rather than arguing, you talk about why you need the orange and uncover the underlying interests behind your respective positions, you will discover that one orange can satisfy both of you.

AIM FOR JOINT GAINS
Instead of limiting the thinking to only one or two options, work jointly with the other party to explore many potential solutions creatively.

SEE BOTH SIDES
Assess the situation from the other party's perspective. This improves communication and helps the other party understand how they stand to benefit from the deal.

SEPARATE THE ISSUES
Keep people issues, such as emotions, separate from substantive issues (such as price or delivery dates).

FOCUS ON INTERESTS
Make sure you have a clear understanding both of your own interests and those of the other party.

EXCHANGE INFORMATION
Before making any decisions, exchange information with the other party in order to explore possible solutions jointly.

Conducting interest-based negotiations

KNOW YOUR BATNA
Make sure you have a clear understanding of your BATNA (Best Alternative To a Negotiated Agreement)—the best option available to you if the negotiation process falls apart.

USE STANDARDS
Base your negotiation on precedents, laws, and principles, rather than arbitrary judgments. This makes the agreement fair and makes it easier to explain the rationale to others.

Negotiating from the whole brain

We all think differently, and naturally bring our own "style" to the negotiating table. Understanding the strengths and weaknesses of your thinking style, and tailoring your approach to take into account the style of your counterpart, can greatly improve your success in negotiation.

Understanding your own style

Ned Herrmann, author of *The Creative Brain*, proposed that there are four thinking styles—the rational self, the safekeeping self, the feeling self, and the experimental self—that relate to dominance in different quadrants of the brain. Negotiating is a whole-brain task, requiring the ability to be diligent and rational (quadrant A activities), to plan and organize well (quadrant B activities), to interact well with others (a quadrant C trait), and to be bold and take risks (a quadrant D characteristic). However, only four percent of the population is dominant in all four quadrants. Most negotiators, therefore, have strengths and

✔ CHECKLIST UTILIZING THINKING STYLE DIFFERENCES IN NEGOTIATION

	YES	NO
• Have you determined what your own thinking style is?	☐	☐
• Have you identified your weaknesses in negotiation and are you working to improve in those areas?	☐	☐
• If putting together a team of negotiators, have you taken each person's thinking style into account? Do they complement one another?	☐	☐
• Are you able to quickly assess the thinking style of others?	☐	☐
• Do you take your counterpart's thinking style into account when negotiating with them?	☐	☐

weaknesses in performing the negotiating task and should work to improve in their weakest areas. A negotiator who has limited abilities in the feeling self (quadrant C), for example, can improve by developing his or her emotional intelligence. A negotiator who has limited abilities in the experimental self (quadrant D) can improve by developing his or her creative abilities by taking creativity workshops.

Influencing others

The whole-brain model can sometimes help you influence your counterpart negotiators. For example, if you believe your counterpart's strength is in the feeling self (quadrant C) and their weakness is in the rational self (quadrant A), you will be more successful if you connect to him or her emotionally by building the relationship, and not by trying to connect cognitively through long speeches or rational arguments.

The four types of thinking style

A
THE RATIONAL SELF
Individuals with brain dominance in quadrant A tend to be logical, analytical, fact-oriented, and good with numbers.

B
THE SAFEKEEPING SELF
Individuals with brain dominance in quadrant B tend to be cautious, organized, systematic, neat, timely, well-planned, obedient, and risk-averse.

C
THE FEELING SELF
Individuals with brain dominance in quadrant C tend to be friendly, enjoy human interactions, engage in open communication, express their emotions, enjoy teaching, and are supportive of others.

D
THE EXPERIMENTAL SELF
Individuals with brain dominance in quadrant D tend to think holistically and see the big picture. They are also often creative, comfortable with uncertainty, future-oriented, and willing to take risks.

Creating win–win deals

Some negotiators talk about wanting to create win–win deals, but when they hit major roadblocks leave the negotiating table prematurely, thus missing out on an opportunity to make a good deal. Effective negotiators utilize techniques to make sure that they can create win–win deals.

TIP

SHOW THE WAY

If you are dealing with a win–lose negotiator who thinks the idea of win–win deals is naive and unrealistic, show them how to create value and reach superior agreements by focusing on interests and bundling issues together.

Getting the conditions right

Effective negotiations, unlike competitive sports, can produce more than one winner. However, it takes motivation by both parties to find creative alternatives that fulfill their interests to create a win–win outcome. To promote win–win deals, effective negotiators focus on both the substantive issues of the deal (price, terms of payment, quality, and delivery schedule) and on formulating a social contract between the negotiators—the spirit of the deal. This involves setting appropriate expectations of how the deal will be negotiated, implemented, and revisited, in case future disputes arise. If, in contrast, negotiators believe negotiations are a zero-sum game that must inevitably be won at the expense of the other party, a win–win deal is not possible.

Bundling the issues

Effective negotiators do not negotiate one single issue at a time because this implies there is a fixed pie and only leads to a win–lose scenario. Instead, they bundle several issues together. Trade-offs can then be made between negotiators because negotiators do not place equal importance on every issue. The principle of bundling issues involves placing an issue that is of high value to you (for example, price) with another you consider to be of low value (for example, warranty). When you trade off on issues, you can then keep your high-value issue (price) and give your low-value issue (warranty) away to the other party. The other party, in return, will allow you to have your high-value issue, because your low-value issue is, in fact, of a high value to them. If your low-value issue is also considered to be a low-value issue by the other party, then they will reject the trade-off. Therefore, it is important for you to know what the other party considers to be their high-value issues.

Capitalizing on risk

You can also capitalize on differences in risk tolerance. Some negotiators are more comfortable with high-risk situations than others. As a win–win and risk-taking negotiator, it is possible for you to design a deal where you assume more risk and receive more benefits while your counterpart, who is also a win–win negotiator but risk-averse (avoider), assumes a lower level of risk but receives fewer benefits from the deal.

WIN–WIN NEGOTIATING

FAST TRACK	OFF TRACK
Negotiating on multiple issues simultaneously	Negotiating on only one issue at a time
Understanding what is important to the other party	Focusing exclusively on your own interests
Identifying and leveraging differences in the interests of and the risks to the other party	Ignoring differences in your counterpart's interests and risks

Building relationships

Contract negotiators are typically task-oriented and pragmatic, tend to focus on negotiating specific issues, and do not invest in building relationships. Relationship negotiators, by contrast, invest first in building good relationships before negotiating on specific issues. Effective negotiators need to be skilled at both approaches.

Making a personal connection

Today, more and more Western negotiators value what the Asian, Arabian, and Latin societies recognized thousands of years ago—the value of good relationships. Experienced negotiators invest in building relationships because good relationships "oil" the negotiation process and make it more efficient. For example, Former US Secretary of State James Baker has stated he has seen this occur time and again—once negotiators have a good relationship, even the most difficult and conflict-inducing issues have been resolved, simply because the negotiators were more transparent and flexible with each other.

Making contact

Effective negotiators know that, in the long run, good relationships are best built through face-to-face interaction rather than by talking on the telephone or corresponding via email. Where possible, try to create opportunities to socialize with the other party before the negotiations begin. This is not to talk about the negotiations and "discover secrets," but rather to get to know the other person better and connect with them on a human level. The atmosphere of the negotiation process may be very different if you are not meeting your counterpart for the first time at the negotiation table.

CASE STUDY

Being prepared
When US businessman Robert Johnson was looking for investment to enable him to create a new cable channel, Black Entertainment Television, he did his homework. Before pitching the idea to John C. Malone—one of the industry's biggest players—he learned about Malone's business philosophy of believing in the entrepreneurial spirit and of individuals helping themselves rather than relying on others. When they met, Johnson was able to connect with Malone by highlighting their shared business values. This similarity provided a positive start for their successful business negotiations.

Interacting informally

In your interactions with the other party, take advantage of any opportunities to genuinely express your appreciation and congratulate them for their achievements. Use small talk and humor where appropriate—taking opportunities to interact informally will help you build a relationship. Be cautious, however, and use "safe humor" in order not to risk offending the other party. Where possible, focus on the common ground between you. You may find that similarities are personal (the same hobby, for example) or ideological, such as a similar business philosophy. Such findings offer a solid start for building a long-lasting, friendly, and constructive relationship.

Thinking long-term

You should also protect the "face," or dignity, of others and treat them with respect when you are taking more from a deal than they are. This is especially helpful when you are trying to build long-term relationships. In team negotiations, it can work well to include socially skilled negotiators in your team who can take greater responsibility for building lasting relationships, while others (contract negotiators) focus more on the specific issues.

Developing mutual trust

Trust is an essential component of success in all types of negotiation, whether business, diplomatic, or legal. Ambassador Dennis Ross, former US Coordinator of the Middle East, has stated that the ability of negotiators to develop mutual trust is the most important ingredient of successful negotiation, and that without it negotiations fail.

TIP

TREAD CAREFULLY
Although there are many benefits to a trusting relationship, it is not always possible to build trust. Some individuals and groups are simply not trustworthy, so be cautious in your efforts to develop trust.

Understanding the benefits

Trust involves a willingness to take risks. It has to do with how vulnerable one is willing to make oneself to a counterpart. There are many benefits to having trust between negotiators—it promotes openness and transparency, and makes the negotiators more flexible. Negotiators who trust each other take each other's words at face value and do not have to verify their statements. This reduces emotional stress and other transaction costs, and makes the negotiation process more efficient. The likelihood of achieving good and lasting agreements is also higher.

Keeping your commitments

Building trust is difficult but losing it is easy, especially if you break your commitments. The French diplomat Francois de Callier, who wrote the first negotiation book in 1716, stated that a relationship that begins with commitments that cannot be maintained is doomed. Shimon Peres, the President of Israel, has said promises have to be delivered, otherwise one's reputation is at stake. Although people do sometimes make genuine mistakes and promises in good faith that they ultimately cannot keep, if you want to build trust, you need to make every effort to keep your commitments.

Building your reputation

One of the most important currencies negotiators have is their reputation. It may sometimes be tempting to maximize short-term gains by overlooking the long-term consequences, but experienced negotiators know people prefer to do business with those they trust and guard their reputation fiercely.

Developing trust

Reciprocation is important for building trust. When negotiators offer information or concessions, they expect the other party to reciprocate. Without reciprocation, no further gestures of goodwill will be offered. With reciprocation, the negotiating parties will be able to find ways to collaborate and create value for both.

It is also important to be seen to be fair. Fairness is a subjective matter, however, so make sure you understand the standard of fairness your counterpart adheres to. Past behavior is often used as a predictor for future behavior, so try to behave consistently.

Examples of actions used by negotiators to build trust

When Henry Hollis sold the Palmer House in Chicago to Conrad Hilton, he shook hands on Hilton's first offer of $19,385,000. Within a week Hollis received several offers more than a million dollars higher. However, he never wavered on his first commitment.

In 1873, US financial markets were in poor shape and "king of steel" Andrew Carnegie needed to cash in a $50,000 investment with J. P. Morgan. Expecting a $10,000 profit, he asked Morgan to send him $60,000. Morgan sent $70,000—the investment had made $20,000 profit.

Negotiating fairly

Fairness is an important characteristic in negotiations. Negotiators need to believe the negotiation process and its outcomes are fair, otherwise they may choose to end the negotiations without coming to an agreement, or fail to put the agreement into action.

Ensuring fairness

There are several categories of fairness that contribute to successful negotiations. Distributive fairness relates to the distribution of outcomes (the splitting of the pie). Negotiators use three different principles of distributive fairness:
• Equality: this states that fairness is achieved by splitting the pie equally.
• Equity: this states that the outcome should relate to the contribution made by each party.
• Needs: this states that, regardless of their contribution, each party should get what they need.

In addition, a negotiator's level of satisfaction and willingness to follow through with an agreement are determined by their perception of the fairness of the procedure (procedural fairness), and also the way they feel they have been treated by the other party (interactional fairness).

Fairness is a subjective issue. When negotiating, if you first define what you consider to be fair, you can then use this "fairness frame" as a bargaining strategy in your discussions with the other party. Alternatively, if you state the importance of fairness at the beginning of the negotiation process, it may encourage the other party to be fair.

CLARITY
Be certain the final decision is clear, without any potential for misinterpretations.

JUSTIFIABILITY
Make sure all parties are able to explain why you are slicing the pie this way to someone else.

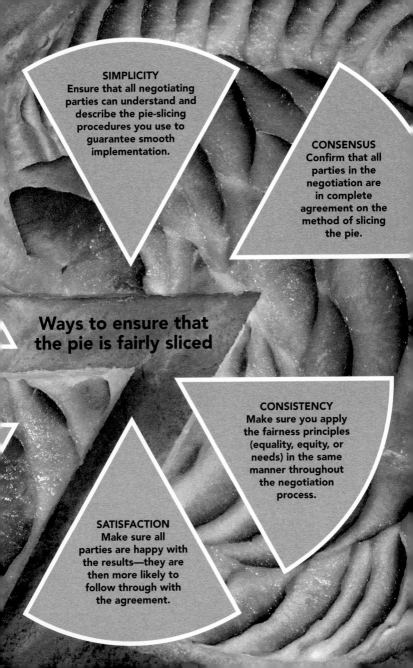

SIMPLICITY
Ensure that all negotiating parties can understand and describe the pie-slicing procedures you use to guarantee smooth implementation.

CONSENSUS
Confirm that all parties in the negotiation are in complete agreement on the method of slicing the pie.

Ways to ensure that the pie is fairly sliced

CONSISTENCY
Make sure you apply the fairness principles (equality, equity, or needs) in the same manner throughout the negotiation process.

SATISFACTION
Make sure all parties are happy with the results—they are then more likely to follow through with the agreement.

Chapter 3
Conducting negotiations

The negotiation process is a strategic interplay between the parties on each side of the table. To be successful, you need to know how to build a strong position, influence your counterpart, deal with difficult situations, and close your deals.

Negotiating with power

Power is a central factor in determining the outcomes of the negotiation process. Effective negotiators understand that power is not static and thus engage in continuously assessing and enhancing it. However, it is equally vital to know how to negotiate when you do not have power.

Understanding power sources

Power can come from a number of different sources:
• **Information** Being well informed enables you to support your arguments and challenge the other party's arguments.
• **BATNA** Having an attractive alternative to a negotiated agreement gives you the power to say "No" to a bad deal and walk away from it.
• **Resources** The party that has more resources—financial, technological, or human—has more power.
• **Needing the deal** The less badly you need the deal, the more power you have not to settle for it.

• **Time** The fewer deadlines you are pressed with, the more power you have to wait and explore opportunities for better deals.

• **Sunk costs** The more willing you are to let go of your sunk costs (such as financial and emotional expenses), the more power you have.

• **Skills** The more skilled you are in the art of negotiation, the more power you have to produce better joint outcomes.

RECOGNIZE YOUR TRUE POWER

Weak parties often underestimate their own power and overestimate that of powerful parties, so try to make an objective assessment of the amount of power you have.

Negotiating from a weak position

If your position is weak, never share this information with the other party. New information or opportunities may arise at any point, which may strengthen your BATNA and your negotiating position. Even if your position is weak overall, try to identify any areas of strength you have and use them as leverage. Even the most powerful party will have some weaknesses, so try to discover these and target them.

Never make "all or nothing" deals from a weak position—you may miss out on opportunities that would have arisen as the value of what you are bringing to the table increases during the negotiation process. Instead, make deals sequentially and in small chunks, to make sure the other party will be more likely to recognize the added value you bring to the table.

USE LIKEABILITY AND INTEGRITY

When in a weak position, do not underestimate the power of personal likability. People do business with people they like and whom they can trust to keep their promises and deliver good value.

CASE STUDY

Creating power

When Thomas Stemberg, the founder of office products retailer Staples, needed a new round of capital to expand his business, he went back to the venture capitalists who had already financed the company. This time, however, they closed ranks and demanded a higher equity share than Stemberg was willing to provide. Determined to break the venture capitalists' cartel, Stemberg sought alternative sources of funding—the pension funds, the insurance companies, and high net-worth individuals—with which he could negotiate from a more powerful position.

Making offers and counteroffers

Before you go into a negotiation, it is vital to plan your opening move. Do you open negotiations and make the first offer or do you wait and allow the other party to go first? Make sure you have an opening offer in mind, and plan how you will respond to your counterpart's offers.

Knowing when to go first

Some experts suggest you should not make the first offer and should always allow your counterpart to go first. Skilled negotiators, however, question the conventional "never open" rule. They choose to tailor their approach to each negotiation. How should you decide whether to go first or second? You should present your offer first when you are confident in the thoroughness of your due diligence and also when you suspect that your counterpart is ill-informed. By going first, you will "anchor," or set a benchmark, that will be used as a reference point for the counteroffer.

If you are not fully informed, do not go first. Consider the other party's first offer, do not respond to it, and do your due diligence. In some cases, two negotiators are equally skilled and well informed and neither wishes to go first. Such cases often require the involvement of a trusted third party to act as a neutral go-between and get the negotiations started.

Setting your offer

Whether you present your offer first or second, how high should your offer be? Former US Secretary of State Dr. Henry Kissinger believes a negotiator is better off starting with a high offer. Most negotiators, however, tend to negotiate first with themselves and thus restrain themselves from making bold offers. They tend to justify their modest offers by thinking their counterparts would not go for a higher offer. Experts today suggest a seller who puts forward a high offer may risk his or her credibility and offend the buyer, who may very well walk away without even providing a counteroffer. Instead of coming up with offers that are either too high or too modest, it is often better to make offers that are bold and daring. Bold and daring offers are reasonably high, tend not to be acceptable, but are still negotiable.

TIP

CONSIDER THE LONGER TERM

If you are hoping to form a long-term relationship with the other party, do not take advantage if they make you a very low first offer. You will generate goodwill and nurture the relationship if you instead respond with a counteroffer that is higher, but still reasonable to you.

IN FOCUS... POSSIBLE RESPONSES TO TOUGH OPENING OFFERS

It is easy to be thrown if the other party's opening offer is extremely low. Effective negotiators make sure they are not startled by a tough first offer, and avoid making a quick, emotional reaction. It is vital that a low opening offer does not become a benchmark for the negotiation. Possible responses to low offers include rejecting the offer as unreasonable; asking the other party to revise the offer; or asking questions and probing the other party for justifications for the toughness of the offer.

Making concessions

Experienced negotiators know that successful negotiations involve a certain amount of give and take, and are well versed in the process of making concessions. They tend to develop offers that leave room for concessions, which are the oil that lubricates the making of a deal.

Conceding in small steps

Each negotiation event is unique, so there are no absolute rules for how to make concessions that apply to all situations. However, it is generally true that people like to receive good news or benefits in installments, rather than all at once. Skilled negotiators, therefore, tend to make multiple small concessions in order to increase the level of satisfaction of their counterparts.

Knowing what to concede

WATCH YOUR TIMING

Think carefully about the timing of your first sizeable concession. If you make it too soon after your initial offer, it will give the other party the impression that the initial offer was not a credible one.

Inexperienced negotiators often make a first sizeable concession as an expression of goodwill. However, this can set the expectation that there are many concessions to be provided. Experienced negotiators, by contrast, tend to untangle the relationships from the concessions. Sometimes, in order to set the tone of reciprocating concessions, they concede first by making a concession on a minor issue.

Wait before you make the first sizeable concession. During this time, advocate for your initial offer and convey the idea that it is not that easy to make concessions. The second concession should be smaller in size than the first and be a longer time in coming. Making concessions in progressively declining installments will then lend more credibility to when you finally say: "There is no more to give."

ENABLING RECIPROCITY

Label the concessions you make as ones that are costly to you and then reduce your value. This sets up the expectation that you will receive a concession in return, implying value for value.

USING CONTINGENCY

If you suspect your concession will not be reciprocated, offer a concession contingent on the other party providing a concession in return. For example: "I will be willing to extend the terms of payment to 45 days if you will increase your order by 500 items."

SETTING BOUNDARIES

Some negotiators put the deal at risk by asking for too much. Set boundaries for the other party by being clear and precise about what you can concede and what you absolutely cannot.

SETTING RULES

Sometimes negotiators make final concessions but then withdraw them or make them contingent on receiving a new concession. Set a clear rule that a concession cannot be withdrawn, unless it was explicitly offered as a tentative or conditional concession.

IDENTIFYING DEAL BREAKERS

Some concessions are deal breakers: if they are not offered, your counterpart will walk away from the negotiation table. Try to distinguish these from value-enhancing concessions, which are demands designed to get a better deal, but if not provided, would not result in the other party abandoning the negotiations.

Being persuasive

A successful negotiation process requires effective persuasion. When attempting to influence your counterpart, it is crucial to identify your moments of power and take advantage of them. Seasoned negotiators understand how to use appropriate persuasion techniques to sell their ideas to the other party.

Influencing others

Effective negotiators use a range of persuasion techniques that take advantage of the natural responses of negotiators to certain types of information. For example, negotiators are generally more motivated to avoid losses than they are to obtain gains. A group of home-owners in California was given the advice that "if you insulate your home, you will gain 50 cents a day." Another group was told that "if you fail to insulate your home, you will lose 50 cents a day." More home-owners under the second set of instructions insulated their homes than under the first set of instructions. Similarly, you are more likely to persuade the other party of the benefits of your deal if you emphasize what they would lose if they don't agree, not what they could gain if they do.

Making small unilateral concessions can be a successful way to influence your counterpart. Negotiators feel obliged to reciprocate, no matter how big or small the concessions are. Even a small concession on your part can help the other party comply The more beneficial your concession is to the other side, the more likely they are to feel obliged to return the favor.

USE SCARCITY
It is human nature for people to want more of what they cannot have. When you present your offer to the other party, inform them of the unique benefits you are offering that they would not be able to get elsewhere.

GAIN COMMITMENT
Encourage the other party to agree to an initially modest request. They are then more likely to follow up with their commitment by agreeing to your key demand to justify their past decision to say yes to you.

Strengthening your hand with persuasion techniques

GIVE "SOCIAL PROOF"
People often use "social proof" when making decisions—they think that if many people are doing things a certain way, it must be good. Demonstrate how your product or service has been successfully used by others.

LET THEM SAY "NO"
Give the other party the opportunity to say "No" by making an outrageous demand, before retreating immediately and putting forward a reasonable demand. This can also serve to make the other party feel obliged to make a concession.

GIVE A REASON
People are much more likely to agree to a demand if you have given legitimate justification for it. Try to give a reason that can be backed up with evidence, but using even a frivolous reason increases your chances of reaching agreement.

SET A BENCHMARK
Negotiators who are not fully informed tend to compare the cost of an item to a reference point or benchmark. You can influence the way they make their decision by setting a benchmark for them.

Managing impasses

Negotiations do not always conclude with an agreement. You may encounter an impasse or a deadlock during the process. How should you deal with a deadlock? Should you leave the negotiation table, concluding that the process has failed, or should you encourage yourself and your counterpart to remain at the table and keep the negotiations going?

Dealing with a deadlock

Skilled and experienced negotiators expect there to be impasses in the negotiating process. They anticipate deadlocks and develop counteractions to deal with them when they occur. They view an impasse as a natural ingredient in negotiations and do not give up easily in their attempts to reach an agreement.

Impasses usually generate negative emotions and sometimes deep feelings of resentment. Prior to and during the negotiation process, you have to be sensitive to the other party's concerns, feelings, and, particularly, their self-image. Research has suggested negotiators have an image to uphold and negotiations are less likely to be successful when either or both parties are not sensitive enough to each other's dignity, or "face." You should always be mindful not to harm the self-image of your counterpart, and never more so than during critical moments of an impasse.

Greasing the wheels

If you are facing an impasse, experts suggest that, in the intensity of the moment, you should first take time out to cool down. This will help defuse the emotional situation and you can resume the discussion at a later time.

Once you reconvene, start by trying to highlight any existing mutual benefits. Impasses usually occur after some progress has already been made. It can therefore be useful to frame the impasse in the context of what has already been achieved—the gains—and highlight the potential losses to both parties if agreement is not reached.

If you are still deadlocked, you may need to try expanding the pie. If you maintain a zero-sum, fixed-pie mentality toward the negotiation, this will restrain your creativity in negotiating for the best deal. Consider that the purpose of negotiation is not to win an argument, but to find satisfactory solutions that would maximize the benefits for both parties. Take the time to generate possible new ideas that could help you reach agreement. Expand the issues you are discussing, but refrain from making concessions. In this way, you may be able to overcome the impasse on one critical issue by adding another issue that is attractive to the other party.

MANAGING DEADLOCK SITUATIONS

FAST TRACK

OFF TRACK

FAST TRACK	OFF TRACK
Anticipating potential impasses and planning in advance how to deal with them	Believing you can just think on your feet if a problem arises
Being open-minded and flexible, and finding creative solutions	Thinking that deadlocks always lead to "no deal"
Reacting calmly and using your emotional intelligence, because you know deadlock situations can be resolved	Leaving the negotiating table early because you are deadlocked with the other party

Avoiding decision traps

Most negotiators believe they are rational. In reality, many negotiators systematically make errors of judgment and irrational choices. It is important for you to understand and try to avoid making these common errors because they lead to poor decision-making.

WATCH YOUR TIMING

To keep from feeling that you have not made the best possible deal, never accept the first offer, even when it is a great offer. Always negotiate a little.

Making the right decisions

Understanding the decision traps negotiators can fall into will help you avoid making the same mistakes yourself, and may allow you to use the other party's errors to leverage your own power. To avoid decision traps or use them to your advantage:

• Do not hesitate to reverse your original decision and cut your losses; create an exit strategy even before you get involved in the negotiation process.

• Take the opportunity to set a benchmark that could give you an advantage when your counterpart is ill-informed, but be aware they could do the same to you if you yourself are not fully informed.

• Engage a trusted expert who will challenge your overconfidence in your ability to negotiate and put pressure on you to do a reality check.

• Make sure your offer is based on solid research. When buying, equip yourself with some security by demanding a performance guarantee of the product.

• Invest time and energy in looking for information that is not easily available. You will often find accessible information that can improve your position.

• Present information more or less vividly to influence others, but be wary of overvaluing information that is attractively presented to you.

• As a negotiator, be aware of how the other party frames the situation and presents its offers.

• Approach each negotiating event as a unique case. They are never identical.

UNDERSTANDING DECISION ERRORS

ERROR	DESCRIPTION
Irrational escalation of commitment	• Acting contrary to your self-interest by increasing your commitment to an original decision, despite the fact that this decision produces negative outcomes ("throwing good money after bad").
Anchoring and adjustment	• Using a faulty anchor as a benchmark from which to make adjustments and decisions. An ill-informed home-buyer, for example, may use the seller's asking price as an anchor for their counteroffer, rather than solid due diligence on home values.
Overconfidence	• Believing you are more correct and accurate than you actually are. This leads to an overestimation of your power within the negotiation, the options open to you, and the probability of your success.
The winner's curse	• If you settle quickly on a deal when selling, feeling that the "win" was too easy and you could have gotten more from the deal. • If you settle quickly on a deal when buying, thinking "I could have gotten this for less" or "What is wrong with this item? I must have gotten a bad deal."
Information availability bias	• Making a decision based on limited information, even though information is readily available or would have been available if enough effort had been put into finding it.
Vividness bias	• Recalling and assigning more weight to information that was delivered in a vivid fashion, and giving less weight to equally important, but dull, information.
Framing and risk	• Making decisions based on how the issues were framed (for example, a glass may be described as being half empty or half full). Risk-averse negotiators are more likely to respond positively to offers that are framed in terms of losses, for example, because they are afraid of losing out; risk-seeking negotiators, in contrast, will respond slowly, because they are willing to wait for a better offer.
Small numbers bias	• Drawing a conclusion based on a small number of events, cases, or experiences, believing that your limited experience allows you to generalize from it.

Managing emotions

In the heat of a negotiation, the emotions you display can significantly influence the emotions of the other party. Effective negotiators try to synchronize their behavior with the other person's, developing an interpersonal rhythm that reflects a shared emotional state.

Understanding the approaches

There are three types of emotional approach in negotiations: rational (having a "poker face"); positive (being friendly and nice); and negative (ranting and raving). Some negotiators believe exposing their emotions to the other party makes them vulnerable and will result in them giving away too much of the pie, and so try to always keep a "poker face" when they are negotiating. They also believe emotional displays may result in an impasse or in defective decision-making, or cause negotiations to end.

Other negotiators believe displaying positive emotions enhances the quality of the negotiated agreement because a good mood promotes creative thinking and innovative solutions to problems, and smoothes out communication. Negotiators with a positive approach use more cooperative strategies, engage in more information exchange, generate more alternatives, use fewer hard tactics, and come to fewer impasses than negotiators with a negative or rational mood.

Q IN FOCUS...
STRATEGIC USE OF ANGER

Some negotiators successfully use displays of anger strategically to try to encourage the other party to agree to their demands. They aim to gain concessions from their opponent because the other party interprets their anger as a sign they are close to their reservation point. Inducing fear in their opponent pushes that person to cave in and agree. It sends the signal they would rather walk away from the table without reaching an agreement than settle for less than what they want. The opponent may also wish to end the unpleasant interaction sooner by giving in.

Being negative

Negotiators who use the negative approach display anger, rage, and impatience in order to influence the other party. Anger is sometimes used strategically, but negotiators who are genuinely angry feel little compassion for the other party and are less effective at expanding and slicing the pie than positive negotiators. They tend to achieve fewer win–win gains when angry than when they experience positive emotions. Angry negotiators are also less willing to cooperate and more likely to seek revenge.

Of the three emotional strategies, the positive and rational approaches are more effective than the negative approach in achieving targets in an ultimatum setting. The positive approach is more helpful in building a long-term, constructive relationship than the rational or negative methods.

Using emotional intelligence

When negotiators are emotionally overwhelmed, their mental capacity to negotiate effectively is impaired. To overcome this, you must manage your emotions intelligently. You need to be aware of the emotions you are experiencing and be able to monitor and regulate them, and you need to find ways to empathize with the other party. For example, when the US Secretary of State James Baker was negotiating with Hafez al-Assad, President of Syria, he had to make a conscious attempt to modulate his irritation. Although he was very angry when President Assad retracted from an earlier commitment, he used the term "misunderstanding" rather than openly displaying his anger.

ASK YOURSELF... DO I USE EMOTIONAL INTELLIGENCE WHEN NEGOTIATING?

- Am I able to make an emotional connection with my counterpart, even if I do not know them very well?
- Am I able to judge when my own emotions threaten to affect my ability to make rational decisions?
- Can I manage my emotions to ensure I am always effective?
- Am I able to react in a measured way, keeping my emotions under control, even if the other party is using value-claiming tactics or behaving in a manner I do not agree with?

Dealing with competitive tactics

In competitive win–lose position-based negotiations, negotiators use various manipulative tactics to maximize their interests while disregarding the interests of their counterparts. They usually believe these tactics are quite effective. Often, however, these tactics can backfire, escalating the level of negotiation or even leading to an impasse. Skilled negotiators recognize these tactical traps and know how to avoid and neutralize them.

Competitive tactics and how to avoid them

MAKING A HIGHBALL OR LOWBALL OFFER

A negotiator assumes you are not fully informed and tries to take advantage by making a very high offer as a seller, or a low offer as a buyer. Their objective is to replace the benchmark you have in your mind with one in their favor.
TO AVOID: Be confident in your benchmarks and try to see clearly through this ploy.

PLAYING GOOD GUY/BAD GUY

One negotiator plays tough and uses aggressive tactics, such as threats and ultimatums. Another empathizes to make you believe he or she is on your side. Neither is on your side—both are trying to maximize their own interests.
TO AVOID: Focus squarely on protecting your own interests.

SEPARATING THE ISSUES

A negotiator insists on reaching an agreement on a single issue before moving on to the next issue. This prevents you from bundling issues together and creating opportunities for trade-offs.
TO AVOID: Negotiate multiple issues at once, stating that "nothing is agreed on until everything is agreed on."

NIBBLING

The deal is done, but at the last minute the negotiator asks for another small concession. Most negotiators concede, fearing that the last-minute demand might derail the deal if it is not fulfilled.
TO AVOID: Remember that refusing to budge on a small concession at the last minute is not usually a deal breaker.

APPLYING TIME PRESSURE

The other party uses the pressure of time to try to get you to concede by setting tight deadlines for an offer, or using delaying tactics to reduce the amount of time available for the negotiation.
TO AVOID: Use your judgment to decide whether a deadline is real or not.

USING EMOTIONAL BLACKMAIL

A negotiator tries to intimidate or influence you by fabricating anger, frustration, or despair. They try to emotionally shake you and make you feel responsible for the lack of progress.
TO AVOID: Use your emotional intelligence. Stay calm and centered and try to steer the negotiations back on track.

Closing the deal

Closing the deal after reaching an agreement is the last but most critical part of any negotiation process. It is certainly not simple, and is not just about outcomes. It also has to do with building relationships and making sure the negotiated agreements can be carried out smoothly. Closing the deal properly is especially important when negotiated agreements are complex and multidimensional.

Preparing to close

Before you close the deal, both you and your counterpart need to understand that the purpose of making the deal is not to sign the contract, but rather to accomplish what the contract specifies. What goals is each party pursuing through the deal and what will it take to accomplish them? Because you depend on each other to accomplish your goals, it is important to make sure both parties are signing the contract wholeheartedly. Review both parties' key interests and make sure nothing has been neglected. It is quite possible for the other party to decide to overturn the entire deal if he or she feels pushed into an agreement without having their own needs met.

CHECKLIST **CLOSING A DEAL**

	YES	NO
• Have you considered all possible stakeholders?	☐	☐
• Have you clarified the purpose of the deal?	☐	☐
• Have you made sure both parties understand what it takes to implement the agreement?	☐	☐
• Have you built a relationship with the other party, to pave the way for future collaboration?	☐	☐
• Have you made enough arrangements for another team to implement the agreement, if another team is taking over?	☐	☐

Considering implementation

Most negotiators underestimate the importance of implementation. If not considered, the intense process of negotiation can undermine your ability to achieve your goals after the deal has been signed. For example, if you have used hard negotiation tactics to push the other party to agree to the deal, the other party may feel, upon signing the contract, that they have been unfairly treated and sabotage the deal, or fail to deliver.

Before you put pen to paper, discuss the implementation of the deal with the other party. What you agree must fulfill the needs of both parties if you are to ensure successful implementation. Unless both parties have confidence the deal can be successfully implemented, there is no point in continuing the discussion.

Reaching agreement

A written agreement usually marks the closure of a negotiation. The agreement, which includes solutions for both parties, may be summarized and you may ask the other party to sign this document. This is the most simple and natural way to conclude a negotiation.

HOW TO...
ENSURE EFFECTIVE IMPLEMENTATION

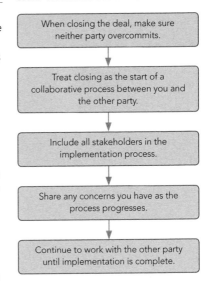

When closing the deal, make sure neither party overcommits.

Treat closing as the start of a collaborative process between you and the other party.

Include all stakeholders in the implementation process.

Share any concerns you have as the process progresses.

Continue to work with the other party until implementation is complete.

Changes should be allowed after the agreement has been signed. In other words, if circumstances change, both parties should feel comfortable contacting the other party to discuss these changes. Upon mutual agreement, such changes can be incorporated into the new agreement. Make sure you include this last point in the agreement because a deal is not done until it is done. It is better to allow for some flexibility than to force the other party to overthrow the entire deal, should the circumstances change.

Chapter 4

Developing your technique

However experienced you are at negotiating, there are always ways to improve your technique. Negotiating in groups, in an international arena, and using your skills to mediate conflicts all require a tailored approach to achieve the best results.

Negotiating as a team

Many business situations are too complex for a solo negotiator to be fully informed about every aspect of the deal. In such cases, working in a team may give better results, though this requires a high degree of internal coordination and a smooth flow of information between members.

Deciding when to use a team

Some negotiations demand a diverse set of abilities. In addition to sound negotiation and psychosocial skills, you may need specific technical expertise, for example, in areas of law, drafting joint ventures, or the planning system. You may need to exercise leverage on your opposite number through the use of PR, or require a keen appreciation of strategy and politics in order to identify the multiple stakeholders in the negotiation and figure out their interests. If you lack any of these abilities, you will probably benefit from the collective wisdom of a team.

Understanding the advantages

There are many benefits to negotiating as a team. Being part of a team provides for multiple creative trade-offs and options and has other advantages, too. Sheer "strength in numbers" makes a team feel secure and powerful and sends a clear message to the other party that you are serious about the deal. You are also likely to feel less pressured when negotiating as a team, and unlikely to make too many concessions too early in the process.

TIP

MAKE TIME TO PREPARE

Make sure you have enough time to create a cohesive, trustworthy team, and allow time to prepare your strategy as a group before you enter into a team negotiation.

Avoiding the pitfalls

Working in a team can lead to a lack of focus and consistency, so appoint a chief negotiator to lead your team and agree in advance on each member's role and responsibilities. Avoid falling into "groupthink," when team members feel pressured to conform to an existing group mindset and reluctant to present ideas that conflict with it. It can also be easy for a team to create a false sense of cohesiveness: "us," the good team, versus "them," the bad team. If this happens, genuine conciliatory attempts made by the other party can be dismissed as dishonest "tricks" and rejected, resulting in missed opportunities to make a deal.

IN FOCUS... DECISION TIME

Negotiating as a team begs the question of how to decide on a course of action. Broadly, there are three ways to reach a decision: first is unanimity, in which all team members must agree on a given issue. This is a tough rule and not recommended for most situations. Second is the majority rule. The majority will decide and the minority will comply with the decision. The hazard here is that the majority may impose a tough solution the minority cannot live with. The third, and usually best, decision-making rule is consensus: making a decision not all the team members agree with fully, but that all can live with.

Dealing with many parties

Many business partnerships or deals involve agreements between three or more different parties, each with their own positions, needs, and goals. Negotiating in this environment requires dexterity and a constant eye on the pitfalls, such as coalitions between the parties opposing you.

Balancing complex issues

Multiparty negotiations are in many ways similar to two-party situations but require a wider set of skills to deal with their additional complexities, which include:

• **Informational complexity** The number of parties involved produces multiple exchanges of information, proposals, and multiple trade-offs. You need to develop a solid information system that can record and recall all the information exchanged in the negotiation room.

• **Strategic complexity** Multiple parties have many interests, and often conflicts of interest, between them. Each party has its BATNA (Best Alternative to a Negotiated Agreement), which may change as alliances are formed. To be well prepared for a multiparty negotiation, you must constantly reassess your own and your counterparts' BATNAs.

CASE STUDY

Chairing multiparty talks

The central challenge for the Chair of a meeting is to gain the trust of the negotiating parties. Former Senator George J. Mitchell, US Senate Majority Leader, stated that in mediating the dispute in Northern Ireland, his ability to be effective ultimately depended more on gaining the delegates' trust and confidence than on his formal role and authority. The Chair should be clear about his or her role, introduce the agenda, introduce ground rules, provide parties with opportunities to express themselves, and distill common interests. The Chair should also regularly summarize the progress that has been made in the negotiation.

SUCCEEDING IN MULTIPARTY NEGOTIATIONS

FAST TRACK

OFF TRACK

FAST TRACK	OFF TRACK
Forming or joining coalitions	Insisting on acting independently
Resisting group pressure to modify your core interests	Settling too easily when faced by a coalition
Being clear when you disagree	Keeping quiet: silence may be interpreted as assent
Monitoring the positions of all the parties	Focusing on only one part of the negotiations

• **Procedural complexity** The design of the negotiation process may be fraught with difficulty. Its structure—the rules of engagement, the selection of the venue, the sequence of the issues, and how decisions will be made—must be perceived by all parties to be fair. In high-value negotiations, it is wise to employ a trained expert to facilitate the process more effectively.

• **Social complexity** With more negotiators involved, the social context becomes complex. In a two-party negotiation, your focus is on one individual, but multiparty negotiations require you to understand, analyze, and build relationships with each and every negotiator. You must learn to resist excessive social pressure and always protect your interests, even when faced by a coalition of parties in the negotiation.

• **Emotional complexity** Negotiating in a multiparty context can be very taxing. Make sure your emotions are held in check; emotional distress often results in poor decisions.

GAIN POWER

Consider building a coalition if you think you hold a weaker hand than one of your opponents. Being part of a successful coalition may help you shift the balance of power.

Building winning coalitions

The moment there are more than two parties in a negotiation, there are opportunities to make coalitions. To protect your interests and remain in the negotiating game, one of your major objectives is to think well in advance about offence (how to build a winning coalition) as well as defense (how to put together a blocking coalition).

When attempting to build a stable coalition, there are three essential factors to consider. The first is the issue of agreement. Some parties will agree and others will disagree with your vision and the strategies and tactics you plan to use to achieve it. The second is influence. Some potential partners may be highly influential and can use their positions of power to assist you in moving your agenda forward, while others will be weak and unable to help much. The third factor to consider is trust. Coalitions are temporary entities driven by self-interest, so partners are easily seduced to defect once the payoffs elsewhere become higher. Your main objective should be to recruit potential partners who are trustworthy and will remain loyal to the coalition.

DIVIDE THE PIE

Make it clear to your coalition partners how the benefits—the proverbial pie—will be divided if you achieve your goals. The division certainly must be fair, but fairness does not necessarily mean an equal share.

ASK YOURSELF... ABOUT FORMING A COALITION

- What is your agenda for the negotiation and what are you trying to achieve?
- What are the main factors you need to consider in building your coalition?
- Can you identify potential coalition partners who are most likely to work with you to allow you to jointly fulfill your objectives?
- How should you sequence the recruitment of each potential coalition partner?
- What is the best way to approach potential partners?

Recruiting coalition partners

When building a coalition, start by identifying all stakeholders, both supporters and opponents of your objectives. Classify each one according to their level of agreement (high, medium, or low, on a scale from one to 10), the degree of influence they could bring to the coalition, and their level of perceived trustworthiness. First, approach your best potential allies—the parties who agree with your vision and agenda and are very influential and trustworthy. Next, focus on the allies who agree with your vision and are trustworthy, but who do not hold positions of power at the moment; they may gain influence as the negotiation proceeds. Ignore the weak adversaries—those who disagree with your agenda and have little influence. At the same time, think how you could block your powerful adversaries. Can you make a coalition with one of their potential partners?

Coalition partners are often motivated solely by gains. Once the gains elsewhere are higher, they may defect, so you should attempt to cement integrity within the coalition. One way to do this is to ask each partner to make a public commitment to the coalition, making it harder for them to defect.

Negotiating internationally

In today's global economy, ever more business deals are made across national borders. Negotiating international deals is a considerable challenge because you must be familiar with the complexities of the immediate negotiation context, such as the bargaining power of the parties and the relevant stakeholders, as well as the broader context, which may include currency fluctuations and government control.

Understanding the differences

You are likely to experience significant differences in several key areas when you engage in international negotiation:

• **Agreements** Western negotiators expect to conclude the process with a comprehensive bulletproof legal contract. In other countries, and notably in Asia, memorandums of understanding (MOAs), which are broader but less substantial agreements, may be more common.

• **Time sensitivity** In countries in which a "doing" culture is prevalent, people believe in controlling events and managing time strictly. In some countries, time is not viewed as such a critical resource, and negotiations can be slow and lengthy.

• **Degree of formality** Negotiators from informal cultures tend to dress down, address one another by their first names, maintain less physical distance, and pay less attention to official titles. By contrast, negotiators from formal cultures tend to use formal titles and are mindful of seating arrangements.

POLITICAL RISK
While some countries have long traditions of an abundance of resources and political stability, others have scarce resources and are marked by volatile political changes.

IDEOLOGY
In individualistic cultures like the US, the purpose of the business is to serve the interests of it shareholders, but in collecti cultures, the business has a larger purpose, which is t contribute to the commor good of society.

Factors to consider in international negotiations

POLITICAL AND LEGAL SYSTEMS
Different countries have different tax codes, labor laws, legal philosophies and enforcement policies, laws that govern joint ventures, and financial incentives for attracting business investments.

BUREAUCRACY
Business practices and government regulations vary from country to country. In some countries, the government bureaucracy is deeply embedded in business affairs, and businesses are constantly required to secure government approval before they act.

INTERNATIONAL FINANCE
Currencies fluctuate and affect the balance of expenses and profits. The stability of the currency your investment is made in affects the risk to you. Many governments also control the flow of currency, limiting the amount of money that can cross their borders.

CULTURE
Different cultures have starkly different cultural beliefs about the role of individuals in society, the nature of relationships, and the ways in which people should communicate. These have a fundamental effect on how you need to approach a negotiation.

Negotiating in Asia

Succeeding in any international negotiation means taking the time to understand the complex negotiating environment, being sufficiently flexible to be able to change your ways if necessary, and learning to work within governmental bureaucracies. The cultural and business landscape in Asia is especially unfamiliar to Western organizations, and, with the region's rapid rise to economic prominence, every manager needs to be aware of how it differs.

Acknowledging differences

Asian culture is characterized by concern for people's feelings. It emphasizes interdependence, harmony, and cooperation, while Western culture tends to be more competitive and achievement-oriented and rewards assertiveness.

Asian societies give a higher priority to collective goals; self-sacrifice for the good of the whole is a guiding principle. There is a greater acceptance of unequal power distribution, and relationships are built based on differences of stature, age, and gender.

Another cultural differentiator is the level of comfort of individuals in ambiguous situations. People in business in China and Japan seek to avoid uncertainty, preferring structured and clear situations in which they are able to make decisions after careful evaluation of a large amount of information. Contrast this with some Western societies, where people are more comfortable with ambiguous situations and are prepared to make quick decisions based on a limited amount of information.

Be aware too that there are differences in communication styles: Asians may be "high context" (indirect, implicit, and suggestive), while those from the West are "low context"—more direct and specific.

TIP

MAKE A CONNECTION
Present your partners with a long-term vision of the mutual benefits of a deal, stressing your personal relationship rather than legal obligations.

TIP

BE PATIENT
Indian negotiators are more concerned with getting good outcomes than with the efficiency of the negotiation process, and may negotiate for weeks or even months to get the best deal. Never put pressure on your counterpart to reach an agreement more quickly or you may lose the deal.

The Asian style of negotiation

RELATIONSHIPS ("GUANXI")
Chinese business leaders invest heavily in making interpersonal connections and creating a dependable social network, known as "guanxi." They prefer to do business within their trusted network.

EMOTIONS
The Confucian teaching *xinping qihe*, meaning "being perfectly calm," makes it difficult for Western negotiators to "read" their counterparts and to know where they stand.

FAIRNESS
The concept of fairness is based on needs—those who have more should give to those with less.

TRUST FROM THE HEART
Asian businesses like to do business with trustworthy individuals rather than faceless organizations. The lengthy process of building trust is based on openness, mutual assistance, understanding, and the formation of emotional bonds.

FACE
Dignity and prestige are gained when individuals behave morally and achieve accomplishments. Face is a formidable force in the Asian psyche that negotiators in Western organizations must be particularly aware of.

LEGALISM
You risk insulting your Asian counterpart if you emphasize penalties for dishonoring commitments in detail. Contracts are short and merely a tangible expression of the relationships being created. They are not treated as "fixed" legal instruments.

DECISIONS
Although Chinese and Japanese societies are hierarchical, they use the consensus style of decision-making. Lead negotiators refrain from dictating a decision in order to preserve relationships and give face to others.

Examining the role of gender

Are women better negotiators than men? Research reveals real differences in negotiation styles between the genders, but there are also deep-seated gender stereotypes in many cultures. How these gender differences are handled, by both men and women, is critical in determining the quality of the agreement you reach through negotiation.

Being aware of perceptions

Enthusiastic and thoroughly prepared negotiators, whether men or women, tend to perform better than less-interested and less-committed ones. In an ideal world, in which neither party is concerned about gender, female negotiators can perform just as well as their male counterparts. In the real world, it pays to be aware of the real and perceived differences between the sexes when approaching a negotiation.

Addressing stereotypes

Women are stereotypically portrayed as being at a disadvantage in the negotiating environment. The myths are that, while men behave rationally, women are emotional; where men are assertive, women are passive; and while men are competitive, women tend to prefer a collaborative approach.

As a woman, your attitude toward these stereotypes and how you choose to handle them when negotiating with men plays a critical role in determining the outcome of a negotiation. If you accept the stereotype and feel and appear anxious at the negotiating table, you may confirm the stereotype and trigger a self-fulfilling prophecy of expecting less and getting less. If you acknowledge the stereotype and try hard to overcome it, you will gain an advantage; people are generally prompted to assert their freedom when they feel restricted by others, and using these feelings in a negotiation may serve to make you bolder and more assertive, and help you gain a bargaining surplus.

Men may also be affected by perceived or real gender differences in negotiations. When men negotiate with women, they may either choke under the pressure to overperform, thus leading to a less favorable outcome; or they may feel guilty and fail to take advantage of their male traits, which would also lead to a less favorable outcome.

GENDER DIFFERENCES IN NEGOTIATION

AREA OF ACTIVITY	MALE CHARACTERISTICS	FEMALE CHARACTERISTICS
Setting goals	Tend to set high goals	Tend to set lower goals
Making concessions	Tend to make few concessions	Tend to make more concessions
Splitting the pie	Focus more on outcomes—getting a larger slice of the pie	Focus more on building and maintaining relationships than obtaining an outcome
Accepting offers	Tend to regret their decision later and feel they could have gotten more, especially after accepting a first offer	Tend to feel relieved after accepting an offer

Using a coach

Many negotiators have blind spots, hold false assumptions, and are prone to repeating their mistakes. Some continue to fail to understand the other party's perspective fully, are unable to convert positions to interests, or are unable to manage their emotions. Working with a coach is an excellent way to gain perspective on your weaknesses and strengths and develop your skills for greater success.

Understanding the benefits

Many negotiators do not realize they could improve their techniques. They continue to make the same mistakes because they filter information, hearing only what they want to hear, rather than absorbing the complete information required to perform well. Another self-serving trap is attribution. Negotiators often attribute problems in negotiations to their counterpart negotiators. An objective coach who is willing to challenge you can help raise your awareness of your limitations and improve your performance.

WORKING WITH A COACH

FAST TRACK	OFF TRACK
Embracing coaching as a way to become more successful	Rejecting an offer of coaching, because you can't improve
Respecting your coach's assessment of your weaknesses	Believing your coach doesn't understand your superior approach
Using the feedback your coach gives you to improve your skills	Dismissing your coach's advice, because you know better

Being assessed

When you first work with a coach, he or she will make an assessment of your performance. This often starts with a 360-degree feedback session, in which your coach collects data from people you negotiate with in order to identify your strengths and weaknesses. The coach may also "shadow" you in actual negotiations, to take note of your performance. Witnessing you in action allows a coach to provide relevant and insightful suggestions for improvement. The key outcome from the diagnosis is for the coach to identify your patterns in beliefs and behaviors, so that you have a higher level of self-awareness.

Fine-tuning your style

The coach then works with you to identify the skill sets and attitudes you want to focus on throughout the coaching period. Coaches are experienced in diagnosing possible pitfalls in your negotiation styles and can help you be proactive in preventing them from occurring. They can also help you uncover issues and resolve them on your own. They can expand your repertoire of behaviors by trying out different approaches and styles with you. Coaches ask

IN FOCUS...
ROLE PLAY

Scenario role play can be an effective method of preparing for negotiations. A coach can help you rehearse your role and make sure there are no gaps or weaknesses in your case and in the negotiation process. For example, the coach can help identify your BATNA or make sure you are not too enamored with the potential deal to the extent you are unable to walk away from it. Although it is impossible to script a negotiation process perfectly ahead of time, it is helpful to "know your destination and all the terrain," so that even if the other party takes the process off track, you can still find a way to achieve your goals.

a lot of questions. A good coach helps the negotiator test his or her own assumptions, consider different perspectives, and reach a conclusion about how to proceed. Many will use scenario role play to help you practice new ways of doing things.

Once you have used the new approaches in a real negotiation, a coach can provide a nonthreatening evaluation and help you learn from your mistakes, achievements, and missed opportunities. Your learning can then be applied in your next round of negotiations.

Being a mediator

As a manager, you will often have to negotiate directly with others within your organization, but will also sometimes be asked to get involved as a third party to try and help parties engaged in disputes to resolve their conflicts. You therefore need to understand the principles of effective mediation and how your role is different to that of other mediators.

Defining mediation

Mediation is a structured process in which an impartial third party facilitates the resolution of a conflict between two negotiating parties. For mediation to be successful, the person selected to mediate a dispute must be acceptable to both of the parties. They must be entirely satisfied that the mediator is unbiased and will assess the circumstances of the dispute objectively.

If you are asked to mediate a dispute, you need to be certain you will be able to remain impartial and not let yourself get swept up in the emotional side of what is taking place. Your role will require you to look at the situation from the perspective of each of the disputing parties to find areas of common ground between them and use this information to make recommendations that would be acceptable to both parties.

ENCOURAGE SELF-DETERMINATION
Be sure the disputing parties recognize their differences and know that the participation in the mediation process is voluntary and they are free to leave at any time.

GIVE OWNERSHIP
Let the disputing parties know they must take responsibility for the conflict and for its resolution, and are expected to identify the issues and engage creatively in solving the conflict.

REMAIN NEUTRAL
Make sure you remain neutral and help facilitate the mediation process, rather than actively trying to influence the outcomes of the conflict.

Principles of effective mediation

KEEP THE GOAL IN MIND
Always remember that the goal of mediation through integrative negotiation is not to achieve absolute justice, but to develop options and find the most workable and satisfactory option.

ADVOCATE CONFIDENTIALITY
Make it clear to all parties that the mediation process is confidential. Disputing parties are only likely to share important information if they believe the mediator is neutral and trustworthy.

USE AN INTEGRATIVE APPROACH
Try to understand the interests of each of the disputing parties and help them reach an integrative (win–win) resolution they would both find acceptable.

Remaining impartial

The manager's role as a mediator is similar to that of other neutral third-party mediators. He or she is working to the same goal as other mediators—to help the disputing parties resolve their disputes. However, as the types of conflict a manager has to deal with often affect organizational goals and performance, he or she may sometimes find it difficult to remain neutral to its consequences. In order to protect the organization's interests, the manager may sometimes have to exercise more control over how the conflict is mediated and also over how the dispute will be resolved. In addition, managers will often have a shared history and possibly a future relationship with the disputing parties. Given these challenges, a manager must do his or her utmost to mediate the dispute in an unbiased manner.

Understanding the process

The mediation process is a step-by-step, structured process. However, unlike the rigid legal process used for mediation, the process used by managers is flexible. It involves five main steps:

• **Initial contact** Start by meeting with each party to identify the issues and provide general information about the mediation process and principles.

• **Assessment and preparation** Next, you need to introduce your role as the mediator, and talk to each disputing party to obtain information about the nature of the dispute. You should also make an assessment of your ability to mediate this dispute, by deciding whether the disputing parties are ready for mediation. You also need to get the parties to commit to engaging in constructive mediation, by asking them to sign a contract. Finally, make a list of the issues in dispute for later discussion.

• **Joint opening session** Once you are fully prepared, you then need to establish a psychologically safe environment in which the mediation can take place. Clarify the rules of engagement, such as mutual respect, taking notes, and meeting privately with each disputing party. Educate the parties on the differences between each of their positions and interests and begin to work on the issues.

• **Joint sessions** Facilitate a productive joint problem-solving situation by continuing to move the disputing parties from positions to interests. Prioritize and narrow down the issues, identify areas of agreement and areas of disagreement, and encourage the disputing parties to make realistic proposals. This may take one or a number of sessions.

• **Agreement** Write down aspects of the agreement as the disputing parties begin to agree on more issues. Make sure that the final agreement is very precise, is owned by the disputants, and is forward-looking.

MEDIATING AS A MANAGER

FAST TRACK	OFF TRACK
Making sure the disputing parties reach an integrative agreement that is satisfactory to all	Failing to take the time to listen to and understand fully the interests of the disputing parties
Trying to resolve the conflict as quickly and efficiently as possible	Allowing the conflict to disrupt the organization's day-to-day business
Making sure that the mediation process is fair to both parties	Introducing your own biases
Allowing disputing parties to express their feelings	Disregarding the emotions of the disputing parties

Learning from the masters

Irrespective of the field in which they ply their trade, be it business, law, diplomacy, labor, or sports, master negotiators possess a unique set of combined characteristics that clearly differentiate them from common negotiators, and define their success. Every negotiator can benefit by understanding the skills and attitudes of a master negotiator.

Becoming a winning negotiator

Master negotiators have superior negotiating capabilities in three major areas: the ability to understand and analyze issues (cognitive skills); the ability to manage emotions, especially negative ones (emotional skills); and the ability to connect with others by developing relationships and trust (social skills). These are the areas you need to work on if you are to hone your negotiating skills and work toward becoming a master negotiator.

Defining key attributes

The following characteristics are common to all master negotiators:

• **Using masterful due diligence** Master negotiators understand the dangers of being poorly prepared and invest ample resources in planning and gathering information.

• **Thinking strategically** Negotiations are rarely a one-on-one business, so master negotiators spend time analyzing the interests of the "players" who are not at the table, how the power balance lies, and what opportunities exist to increase their own power.

• **Being firm and flexible** Master negotiators are firm and clear about the issues they must have, and flexible on the issues they would like to have.

• **Seeing the other side** Master negotiators know they can only present a good offer or trade-off if they know what their counterpart's interests are. They are able to shift easily from seeing things from their point of view to seeing things from the viewpoint of the other party.

• **Investing in relationships** Master negotiators use all possible opportunities to nurture trust and develop relationships, and make sure those connections remain intact over time.

• **Managing emotions** Master negotiators make an active choice always to monitor and control their emotions constructively.

• **Appreciating uniqueness** Master negotiators approach every situation afresh and are always ready to modify their practices and adapt to the specific conditions of the current negotiation.

IN FOCUS... BAD DEALS

Master negotiators know that negotiations are not about making the deal and signing the contract, but rather about diligently pursuing their interests. No deal is better than a bad deal, so they condition themselves mentally to walk away from the table if and when their interests are not met. Inexperienced negotiators tend to be biased toward securing a deal and often tend to stay at the table and get a poor deal. There are two reasons for this: first, negotiators do not want to let go of the sunk costs (expenses) involved in attempting to make the deal. Second, they do not want to face the fact that it simply is not possible to make the deal and thus feel they have failed to produce results. Master negotiators, by contrast, are willing to let go of the sunk costs and do not feel they have failed in the negotiation task if the deal does not go through.

PRESENTING

Contents

Introduction

The increasing pace and competitiveness of business makes the need for communication all the more urgent. It is not surprising that presentations have become an essential tool for business communication in workplaces around the world. After all, ideas need to be shared in a clear and convincing way if they are to influence others.

Every presentation is a pitch in which you must sell your ideas to colleagues or outside audiences. This holds true whether your intention is to inform or to persuade, whether you are delivering a formal speech from behind a podium, a presentation using visual aids, an informal address to your staff, or a briefing distributed through the media.

Successful presenters understand what they must communicate, who they are communicating with, and for what reason. With preparation and practice—and working through each of these elements—anyone can learn to plan, assemble, and deliver a successful presentation every time.

The elements of great presentations are described in this guide in practical detail, making it ideal for new managers and experienced communicators alike.

Chapter 1

Planning to present

A presentation is a way of informing, inspiring, and motivating other people. Whether your audience is a group of receptive colleagues, demanding clients, or strict regulators, your job is to influence the way they think and feel about your message. No matter how charismatic you may be, success depends on careful planning of your content and delivery.

Putting the audience first

Presenting successfully means stepping back from your own knowledge of your subject. Examine what you want to say and how you convey that information from the perspective of the audience. Their priorities will almost always be different from yours.

TIP

WATCH YOUR LANGUAGE

Check the language abilities of your audience—if you do not share a first language, you will need to make allowances.

Identifying the need

A presentation serves a very different purpose to a written report—it is far more than just another vehicle for information. A presentation allows an audience to gain knowledge by watching, listening, and being inspired by you. Audiences come not to learn everything you know about a subject, but to gain your perspective—they are likely to remember only the big themes even a short time afterward. Good presenters understand audiences are looking for information in context, not in full detail, so ask yourself what *you* can add through *your* presentation of the subject.

Researching the audience

Get to know your audience, even before you plan your presentation. Talk to the organizer of the event about their expectations, and if possible, engage with those attending ahead of time; ask them about their existing level of knowledge, and what they hope to hear about. Figure out if they need persuading, informing, educating, motivating, or a combination of all these. The more you understand your audience's expectations, the better you'll be able to meet them.

TIP

MATCH THINKING STYLES

Is your audience made up of creative thinkers or analysts? You'll need to tailor your content and delivery to match their thinking style.

Focusing your message

Identify the essential information you want your audience to understand and remember. You should have no more than three such core messages. Build your presentation around these points and add supporting details where necessary—but remember that less is more when it comes to oral presentation. Make your key points emphatically and repeatedly and don't try to be too subtle or clever. Always look for the overlap between what you want to say and what your audience wants to hear.

? ASK YOURSELF... WHO IS MY AUDIENCE?

- Who will be listening?
- What do they already know? Is there a common understanding to build on?
- What are their expectations? Will they hold any preconceived notions about the subject?
- What do I want them to learn? What do I expect them to do with that knowledge?
- What will I say to accomplish my goals?

Presenting and selling

Presentations serve a great variety of purposes. They can be used to inspire and motivate people or they can be designed simply to convey information formally (as in a lecture) or informally (as in a team briefing). But most often, they are used to promote a product, service, or idea, or to persuade stakeholders about a particular course of action. In other terms—whether overtly or covertly—most presentations aim to sell.

TIP

GET TO THE POINT

Engage your audience by addressing what they want to know quickly. Avoid opening your presentation with background about you or your company—when it was founded, where it's located, and so on.

Pitching your ideas

The better you can meet the needs of your audience, the more successful your presentation will be. So when selling anything, from an idea to a product, your presentation should focus on how it will help your audience, how it will solve their problems. Whenever you talk about your idea, product, or service, don't just list its features—express them as benefits.

Throughout your presentation, your audience will be constantly assessing both your trustworthiness and the strength of your "sell." You need to be able to "read" their reactions so you can address their concerns. Successful presenters do this by inviting many questions from the audience and encouraging them to interrupt; the questions and comments from the audience provide vital feedback.

IN FOCUS... THE TWO-MINUTE PRESENTATION

We often encounter people casually—between meetings or in quick conversations at conferences. It pays to develop a two-minute pitch that introduces you, your business, and the unique value you can offer. The pitch should be very easy to understand, describe the solutions you offer, and reflect your passion about what you do. A good two-minute pitch will get you a surprising number of follow-up meetings.

Selling successfully in your presentation

EXPECT TO CLOSE	If the presentation is effective, the decision to buy, or buy in, is a natural next step. Be prepared to ask for some kind of commitment and agree to take immediate action, even if it is only setting up another meeting.
SHOW, DON'T TELL	Visual representations and physical demonstrations bring sales presentations to life. People remember what they see and do for themselves, so be creative.
KNOW YOUR STUFF	To establish your credibility, you need to know a great deal about your product or service. In addition to handling general, predictable questions, be prepared to demonstrate your knowledge in every respect—commercial, technical, and practical.
BELIEVE WHAT YOU ARE SAYING	An animated, enthusiastic presentation is a must. Buyers do not want to buy from someone who doesn't appear fully committed to the product, even if it is relevant to their needs.
SELL BENEFITS, NOT FEATURES	The presentation must center on what matters most to the buyer—general discussion won't do. Talk about specific benefits. How does the product or service help solve a problem or improve a situation?

Presenting formally

In many presentations, you are in control of what you say and how you say it. But be aware that some types of presentation are much more formal, following rules, requirements, timescales, or formats dictated by the audience or by a third party. They include presentations to boards, regulatory bodies, and examination and assessment panels, all of which require high levels of planning and rigorous attention to detail.

TIP

EXPECT TOUGH QUESTIONS

Formal presentations to boards and panels may be met with adversarial questions. Boards may view harsh questioning as perfectly acceptable, so come prepared with robust answers.

Keeping focused

When you are asked to make a formal presentation, always request guidance about what is expected from you—what is the desired length, content, and context of your material. Play safe—don't attempt to be too innovative with the structure, but stick with a tried and tested formula:

HOW TO...
STRUCTURE A FORMAL PRESENTATION

> Introduce the topic, the argument you are about to make, and the conclusion you will reach.

> Develop your arguments clearly and persuasively, justifying what you say.

> Make a conclusion: summarize your main arguments and explain the relevance of the conclusion made; explain why you are confident of your conclusion.

> Facilitate discussion of your presentation; check that everyone has understood exactly how you have arrived at your conclusion.

Keep your presentation concise and limit the detail that you include. If presenting to a board of directors, for example, bear in mind that they don't get involved in day-to-day management and have many demands on their time. Focus on what they really need to know, but make sure you don't withhold anything important—choose your words very carefully to ensure you cannot be interpreted as being misleading.

Preparing to succeed

Before a formal presentation, make contact with people who know the members of the board. Find out everything you can about their backgrounds, concerns, and predispositions. Use what you have learned to prepare your arguments; if appropriate, try to gain advance support for your position with members of the board.

Confidence is another key success factor. You will be expected to take a strong stand and support it with compelling evidence. Handle challenges with calm assurance and keep in mind that it is your position, rather than your personality, that is under attack. Finally, if you are presenting with colleagues, make sure you "get your story straight"—that your materials are consistent.

Being a panelist

Panel presentations are often a feature of conferences. If you are asked to be a panelist, make sure you understand the specific areas or questions you have been invited to address. Find out who is talking before and after you, and what they are focusing on to keep from repeating their content.

Build flexibility into your presentation because time slots often shift to accommodate delays. Make sure you have time to present your key points. If you feel the topic is too complex for the time frame, suggest an alternative.

Following protocol

Some expert panels are very formally structured, with individual members asked to stand and give a presentation on a topic in turn before fielding questions from other panelists or the audience. Others are much looser, with any panelist permitted to interject, add remarks, or pose questions at any time. If the format of your panel is unstructured, always be attentive while others are speaking, don't interrupt others too often, and don't speak for too long. No matter how informal the structure, always take the time to develop your key messages in advance.

Planning the structure

There are many ways to organize your ideas to create an effective and convincing presentation. Sometimes, the content you need to convey will fall more naturally into one type of structure rather than another. There may also be an element of personal preference—you may simply feel more comfortable with one type of structure than another. But however you choose to organize, the end result must achieve your communication goal. In other words, content always dictates form, not vice versa.

Setting out the basics

All presentation structures share three high-level elements: the introduction or opening; the body or main content; and the conclusion or close. Most of your time will be spent delivering the body, but don't underestimate the importance of opening with an introduction that captures the audience's attention, and tying everything together at the close.

QUICK AND EASY STORYBOARDING

Repositionable notes are a useful tool when storyboarding your presentation. Use a note of a different color for each type of element: here, blue for a key message; pink for each proof point that backs up a message; and orange for a visual aid. Reposition the notes to experiment with running order, the balance between "showing" and "telling," and to identify weak sections. Storyboarding is a method of sequencing your ideas that can help you decide how to represent them in a logical and compelling order when planning your presentation. It adds a physical dimension that is extremely useful for organizing and understanding the impact of a presentation using visual aids.

- **The introduction:** Think of your opening as a promise to the audience. It should tell them what they are going to hear, and why it is important. This section needs to get their attention and give them a reason to keep listening.
- **The body:** This is where you deliver on the promise you made in your introduction. Here you present the facts, analysis, explanation, and any comments that fill out your message. Sustain interest by keeping the opening promise in mind, and making sure every element advances that goal.
- **The conclusion:** Your close is the "so what?" of your presentation. Remind the audience of your key points and clearly articulate where they lead, or conclusions that can be drawn. An effective close demonstrates your conviction about the action you are suggesting or the position you hold. While you should spend no more than 15 percent of your presentation time on the close, remember that this will probably be the section your audience remembers most clearly. Whatever you want them to remember, say it now.

TIP

KEEP IT BALANCED

Your structured content should fall roughly into these proportions: 10 percent introduction, 75 percent body, and 15 percent conclusion. Let each section fulfill its function. Don't overload the introduction or bring in new ideas in the conclusion.

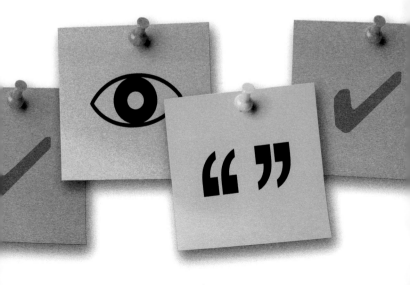

Selecting a framework

To structure your presentation for maximum impact, choose a framework sympathetic to its content. For example, if your material is data-driven, use a numbered list; if you are selling a concept, employ case studies. Described here is a selection of useful structural alternatives.

NUMBERED LIST

Use this model to present modular information such as the top competitors in your market. Quantitative information helps your audience understand the relationship between a list of items.

PROBLEMS AND SOLUTIONS

Outline a problem, then reveal how to fix it. This structure is excellent when discussing change. It can help position you as someone who can read a situation clearly, explain it, and offer a way forward.

FEATURES AND BENEFITS

Work through the elements of a product or proposal and explain the positive outcomes each one can generate. This method works well for more persuasive sales presentations.

DEDUCTIVE OR INDUCTIVE?

Deductive reasoning moves from general principles to specifics ("our market is growing, we should do well"); inductive reasoning moves from specifics to principles ("we've done well, our market is growing").

MESSAGING

Tell them you are going to tell them, tell them, and then tell them you have told them. This simple structure works well provided the messages are clear and backed up with proof.

STORIES AND CASE STUDIES

Present your argument through narrative. People love hearing stories, making this a compelling and forceful presentation method. Keep your story simple and explain the "moral."

COMPARE AND CONTRAST

Put your material in context by comparing it with something else. Make sure your content is coherent and well chosen so similarities and differences are clear to your audience.

OPTIONS AND OUTCOMES

List some choices and the pros and cons of each. Make sure the options are different, not refinements of one idea. If you are going to suggest the best way forward, be prepared to back it up with data.

TIMELINE

A chronological structure is useful for showing progressive developments. Its linear structure is intuitive and easy to understand. To keep from seeming one-dimensional, be sure that your material has both purpose and pace.

Opening and closing

Two simple observations of human interaction will help you plan a powerful presentation. First, you only have one chance to make a first impression; and second, people remember longest what they hear last. These observations suggest that the opening and closing parts of your presentation have particular importance. It pays to practice getting these moments right—making them clear, powerful, and engaging.

TIP

MAKE FRIENDS
Establish a good rapport with the audience early. Greet them warmly; ask them how they are enjoying the day.

Opening powerfully

The opening to your presentation serves many functions. It grabs the attention of your audience, establishes your credibility, and sets the stage for what is to come. Don't begin with an extended introduction, lengthy thanks to your hosts, or a recitation of the agenda—you may not be able to engage your audience after such a slow start. Instead, explain to your audience how listening to you will be of benefit to them, and through your confidence, let them see your competence.

IN FOCUS...
ESTABLISHING YOUR CREDIBILITY

Credibility is everything. Your audience needs to buy into you in order to buy into your message. Introducing yourself (or being introduced) with your academic or professional credentials in specific fields may help, especially at formal or academic conferences, but credibility isn't just a function of title—it is a product of confidence, preparation, and experience. Explain to your audience what experience you bring to the issue and why you are qualified to speak; then show that you understand the information and can apply it independently. In order to keep your credibility throughout, you will need to show you want to communicate, and are prepared to work to do so. You don't have to be word-perfect, but you do need to be focused and organized with what you do know. Your preparation and readiness will speak volumes.

Capturing attention

Be yourself at your most engaging. Rehearse your opening many times—out loud and in front of a mirror—and don't be tempted to improvise. Pump it up, but don't force jokes or stories into the opening if it's not in your character. Most of all, be audience-centered; find common ground with the audience early on. Try using:

- Interesting or entertaining quotes
- Unusual or startling statistics
- Interesting survey results
- Short anecdotes
- Personal stories of experiences or lessons learned
- Outlines of problems and how you would solve them.

Elevating endings

You will probably feel relieved as the end of your presentation approaches, but don't be in a rush to finish because your final words are likely to be those that persist longest in your audience's memory. End with a summary of your key points, or deliver a call to action resting on those points, which will make sure they are remembered. In other words, make sure your ending addresses the objectives you had when starting out.

However you choose to end your presentation, make it meaningful and memorable. Don't end by introducing new ideas you don't have time to support.

TIP

BACK IT UP
Always provide follow-up materials so that you continue your dialogue with the audience. Keep these printed materials concise and relevant to the presentation. Too wide a reach can be off-putting.

CLOSING A PRESENTATION

FAST TRACK

OFF TRACK

FAST TRACK	OFF TRACK
Ending on a positive note, even if you've delivered negative information	Ending abruptly without a summary or call to action, or by calling for questions prematurely
Restating, rather than reexamining, key points in your material	Introducing new information toward the end of your presentation
Being concise	Running out of steam or rushing for the finish line

Winning with words

When you give a presentation, your job is to make the audience understand, recall, and respond to your message. Your success as a speaker depends on your delivery of the message, and this cannot be separated from your choice of words, forms of expression, and the mental images you conjure up as you bring your words to life.

TIP

STAND UP
Whenever possible, present standing rather than seated. You will command attention and gain better control of your breathing and voice.

Convincing and persuading

Persuasive speech, or rhetoric, asks that an audience goes beyond passive listening. Its purpose is to elicit agreement, for example, that a crisis is looming and action is necessary—"to avoid crisis, we must..." The tools of rhetoric were developed in classical times by great thinkers such as Plato and Aristotle, for whom verbal artistry was not just a means to an end, but a way to arrive at truths about politics and justice. Aristotle, for example, relied most heavily on logic to support his arguments, but also recognized the importance of ethos and pathos.

CLASSICAL RHETORIC

TYPE OF RHETORIC	CHARACTERISTICS	EXAMPLE
Ethos	An appeal based on the integrity and reputation of the speaker. You may not understand the reasoning, but you trust the speaker.	"As a leading orthopedic surgeon, I recommend this children's safety seat."
Pathos	An appeal to the emotions of the listener, such as love, compassion, fear, or greed. Often personalizes the argument.	"Give your children the protection they deserve with our safety seats."
Logos	An appeal to the listener based on logic. This would include evidence and reason.	"Fatalities drop by 37 percent with our safety seats. The conclusion is clear."

USING ACTIVE PHRASING

FAST TRACK

OFF TRACK

"Sales are rising. That's better than we expected."	"Surpassing our expectations, sales are rising."
"We're making real progress."	"Progress is being made."
"Training is necessary and it fits our timeline."	"Training, with respect to our current timeline, has been found necessary."
"We can understand complex ideas if they are presented well."	"Complex ideas, provided they're presented well, can be understood."

TIP

MIX YOUR MESSAGE
A rounded presentation combines several different types of arguments—try mixing ethos and pathos in your summing up for a powerful closing.

Creating moments

Beyond the use of clear structure and good narratives, there are many verbal techniques to help your audience remember what you have said. Use these sparingly to emphasize key points. Sprinkling these devices too liberally throughout your presentation will dilute and, therefore, spoil their effect:
• Alliteration: "the sweet smell of success"
• Grouping words in threes: "friends, Romans, countrymen"
• Acronyms: "Audience, Intent, Message—AIM"
• Allegory: "I have a dream"
• Repetition: "Location, location, location"
• Mnemonic: "Thirty days has September..."
• Personification: "This product will be your faithful companion"
• Rhetorical questions: "Can one product really deliver all these benefits?"
• Using a motif: returning to a symbol or visual image throughout your presentation to add continuity.

TIP

HOLD BACK THE PAPERWORK

If you choose to distribute printed handouts to your audience, do so only after you have completed your oral presentation. This will keep the audience from becoming distracted.

Eliminating interlopers

Many speakers insert a word or syllable to fill what they perceive as an awkward gap. These filler words, such as "um" or "ah," arise because we are all used to two-way conversation. When you pause, the other person speaks, and so on. When you are giving a presentation, there is no feedback and the silence can be unnerving. Practice and awareness of your own habits will help you become comfortable with natural pauses while you consider the right phrasing, but knowing your material is the best defense against needing to use unnecessary words to fill a space.

Certain phrases detract from your authority as a speaker. There is a temptation to inject words like "possibly" and "perhaps" to soften what you are saying, so you seem less severe. Don't bother. Eliminating such words and phrases will instantly power up your presentation.

CASE STUDY

The personal touch

Steve Jobs, the cofounder of Apple Computers, is widely renowned for his memorable presentation skills. Jobs often fuels his public appearances and speeches with some personal anecdotes, which allow those outside his industry to understand and be inspired.

"Because I had dropped out and didn't have to take the normal classes, I decided to take a calligraphy class… None of this had even a hope of any practical application in my life, but 10 years later, when we were designing the first Macintosh computer, it all came back to me…. It was the first computer with beautiful typography. If I had never dropped in on that single course in college, the Mac would have never had multiple typefaces or proportionally spaced fonts. And…it's likely that no personal computer would have."

Steve Jobs, Commencement Address, Stanford, California, 2005

Using narrative

Six of the most powerful words in the English language are "Let me tell you a story." Narratives bring facts and figures into context and lift presentations out of the realm of dry tutorials. They provide a showcase for the presenter to demonstrate real passion and grasp of the issues, particularly if the narrative resonates on a personal level. Crucially, like other device, they will captivate the listener.

Learn to use stories effectively, by reading and listening to accomplished storytellers. Draw on your own experiences and practice honing them into stories by telling them in informal situations.

Stories can take diverse forms, but to be useful in a presentation they should have two basic elements—the "what happened," or sequence of events, followed by the "lesson learned" or moral, based on those events.

To further increase the likelihood that your audience will retain your message, distribute a printed handout to supplement your oral presentation. It may be a simple reprise of your presentation; it may contain additional information, elaborating on points you have made; or it may be a list of additional reading. A handout is a useful tool (essential in academic environments), as long as it is thoughtfully structured—it should not just be a place to dump your additional research. Always explain the purpose of your handout to your audience, and never assume it will be read. It is no substitute for your oral presentation.

Introducing visual aids

It is said that a picture is worth a thousand words, and using visual aids in your presentation undoubtedly heightens impact and improves audience retention. In business, the term "visual aid" often reads as shorthand for PowerPoint™ or other presentation software, but you don't need computer technology to add visual flair. A simple prop can make an unforgettable point, and flip charts are foolproof, cheap, and portable.

TIP

BUILD SUSPENSE
Keep a prop covered on the table in front of you before you use it. This will help create intrigue and anticipation.

Preparing to impress

Visuals are of little value unless they clarify and illustrate your message. When planning your presentation, first establish its basic outline; then refer closely to the content to identify the points that would benefit from visual treatment. Consider what kind of visuals will help you communicate your information and where you can use them in your presentation to greatest effect. Will maps help your audience get a handle on locations? Will graphs or pie charts really help them understand figures?

Then consider how much time you will need to invest in finding or generating the visual aids—would your effort be better spent refining and practicing your delivery?

Some visual aids require little or no preparation. Props are objects that help reinforce a point or grab attention and they are particularly useful if you want to evoke an emotional response. Props can also be passed around the audience to engage their senses of smell, touch, and even taste. Use props sparingly, and integrate them well into your presentation so they are not perceived as gimmicks.

IN FOCUS...
RETAINING VISUAL INFORMATION

A study at the University of Pennsylvania's Wharton School of Business found retention rates of verbal-only presentations ran at about 10 percent. Combining verbal with visual messages increased retention rates by nearly 400 percent to 50 percent.

Making images work

The most common presentation tools today are the slide or digital projector, which can carry text and graphics, and the video player. Each needs to be used thoughtfully and sparingly. If you bombard your audience with slide after slide, chances are they will retain very little, and a long video presentation presents the perfect opportunity to grab a nap.

Remember that the audience needs to be inspired and gain your perspective on the subject. You can only provide these yourself.

When using an image to make a point, cut down on narration and allow the audience to discover the message for themselves. Don't talk over a photograph—introduce it. Even a simple photograph of a building will generate more impact than a verbal description alone.

Think very carefully before using a video. Most people are used to high production values and as such anything less could work against you. Customer testimonials work very well as video clips, but if you are planning on using a video element you do need to be selective because the average time allocated for a speech is five to seven minutes. Anything over a couple of minutes of clips and it will appear that your speech is just a distraction for the main event—the video clip!

Using presentation software

Multimedia projection software has become a standard tool for business presentations. Used with care, the software can greatly enhance the impact of your communication, but beware of its seductive nature, which invites you to fill your slides with ever more content and embellishment.

Getting to the point

Creating slides in a dedicated presentation package, such as PowerPoint™ or Keynote™, is easy. But using these tools to communicate effectively is a bigger challenge. First, ask yourself if your presentation will actually benefit from slide formatting; it may be just as effective—or more so—to use props, videos, handouts, or simply your own voice and authority. For example, slides are not the best way to present lots of data (handouts are much better), but they are effective for showing the relationships between sets of data.

Slides are not a magic bullet: they won't organize a disorganized presentation; they won't give a point to a presentation that doesn't really have one; and they'll never make a convincing presentation on their own. What your slides can do is reinforce your points, drawing attention to them as you present.

TIP

KEEP IT SIMPLE
If you find yourself apologizing for the complexity of a slide, take it out.

Choosing the cues

When you elect to use multimedia projection tools, use them for what they are good at—showing rather than telling information. Findings from cognitive scientists suggest that because visual and verbal information is processed separately, audiences have a difficult time absorbing both at the same time. This means you should let images do their own talking, and keep text minimal.

Streamlining your content

AVOID "EXTRAS"
Don't leave your
audience wondering
why you didn't
address something
you put on a slide.

Less is more. Use your slides to emphasize key points
in your presentation rather than as a comfort blanket.
They have far more impact when used sparingly. Don't
include complex charts or graphs, or assume people
will look at your handouts later to decode them. If a
graphic can't be understood during the presentation,
take it out or simplify it. Try breaking it into several
separate slides. It can be very effective to use a series
in which information is "built" with each slide.

Simplify the information on each slide—use no
more than five lines of text per slide, and no more
than six words per line. Some presenters tend to load
their slides with bulleted lists, then deliver their
presentation by expanding on the points, but this
approach fails to engage an audience. Rather than
recapping bullet points, try replacing them with
intriguing keywords that invite your explanation.

WRITING EFFECTIVE SLIDE TEXT

FAST TRACK	OFF TRACK
Using punchy key word bullets, such as: • Revolutionary • Adaptable	Using long bullets or paragraphs of text, such as: • Powered by rotary not conventional engine • Able to work in temperatures of −10° to 50°F
Capitalizing only the first word of each sentence	Using all capitals, excessive underlining, or type effects
Proofreading your text by reading it backward	Using abbreviations or industry jargon

Making great visuals

You don't need to be a graphic designer to produce effective slides. The key—as with text—is to keep things simple, and stick to one, consistent graphic language. Limit yourself to two fonts and two type sizes for the presentation, and use the same conventions throughout, for example, bold text to denote a heading, and italics for quotes. Keep font styles and colors consistent from slide to slide so your audience doesn't have to stop and consider whether any differences are significant to their meaning. Use sans serif* fonts for their clarity and clean lines, and consider using white text on dark backgrounds to reduce glare.

Resist the temptation to present every graphic you have access to. Use no more than two images on one slide, and no more than three separate curves on one graph. Be creative with your images. They don't need to be literal or combined with text. Projecting a single, powerful image will help vary the pace of your presentation and open up discussion.

ASK YOURSELF WILL MY VISUALS WORK?

- Will the type you've used be legible when projected? Colors and sizes may be fine on your computer screen, but not when enlarged by a projector.
- Are image file sizes manageable? Overly large files tend to load slowly and may stall your presentation.
- Is the room dark enough for your slides to be seen? Balance the illumination in the auditorium so you can still see your audience, and vice versa.
- Is the type large enough? A good guide is to add 2in (5cm) of character height for every 20ft (6m) of distance between your slide and the audience.

Sans serif—a typeface that is without serifs (decorations added to the ends of the strokes that make up letters).

TIP

Using conventions

LOOK AT THE AUDIENCE

Don't use your slides as prompts for yourself. It will encourage you to make slides for youself rather than your audience. What's more, it will make you look at the screen, rather than at the audience.

Your audience won't have long to interpret complex graphics, so always simplify to the essentials, and take advantage of familiar visual conventions. For example, use the color red to suggest negative numbers, stop, or danger, use pie charts for relative proportions, and use ascending lines to indicate growth. There is no need to reinvent the wheel. Beware of gimmicks, such as animated transitions between slides. Movement is very distracting when processing information, and such effects should be used sparingly.

HOW TO...
WORK WITH SLIDES

Begin your presentation with a title slide that introduces the topic.

Show slides only when you are talking about them. Don't leave them up.

Spend no more than two minutes addressing a slide.

Direct your audience to a slide using a hand gesture.

Walk your audience through each slide following natural reading patterns (left to right, top to bottom in Western cultures).

When presenting a complex slide, allow the audience some time to absorb the information before you speak.

Presenting virtually

Fast and near-ubiquitous broadband connections have made the delivery of remote, virtual presentations inexpensive and reliable—a far cry from the days when video conferencing involved costly, complex equipment for both the sender and receiver. Getting the best from virtual delivery methods involves combining conventional presenting skills with a new range of techniques.

TIP

CHECK IT WILL WORK

Always check the compatibility of technologies used for conferencing. Some are dedicated applications that must be installed on the users' computers; some are web-based. The presenter may talk over a telephone line, pointing out information being presented on screen, or audio may be incorporated into the software package.

Benefiting from technology

Delivering your presentation online means your audience can watch, listen, and take part from anywhere in the world. It saves time, travel, and expense, and it appeals increasingly to generations of business people for whom the computer has always taken center stage.

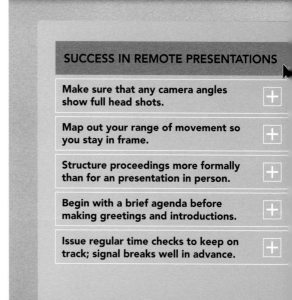

SUCCESS IN REMOTE PRESENTATIONS

Make sure that any camera angles show full head shots. +

Map out your range of movement so you stay in frame. +

Structure proceedings more formally than for an presentation in person. +

Begin with a brief agenda before making greetings and introductions. +

Issue regular time checks to keep on track; signal breaks well in advance. +

Choosing your format

Web conferencing is the direct descendent of video conferencing, allowing live meetings or presentations to take place over the Internet or company intranet. The meeting may be referred to as a webcast, where there is little or no audience participation, or a webinar, where participation is encouraged—via the web, phone, or email. Podcasts can deliver messages that can be viewed on handheld devices or cell phones. All these technologies are increasingly being used to reach staff, investors, and the media, but should always be considered as additions to face-to-face presentation, rather than a replacement. The biggest challenge is keeping your audience engaged when you are not physically present.

Don't overanswer questions. Attention spans in this media tend to be short.

To retain interest, make sure you build in regular feedback breaks.

Try to keep things simple and remind other participants to do so, too.

Use illustrations, graphs, and videos wherever possible.

In audio formats, use repetition to drive home points.

Acknowledge participants and give everyone an opportunity to be heard.

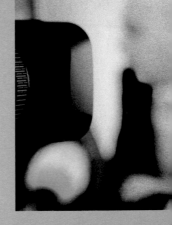

Chapter 2

Preparing and practicing

Every presentation is a performance. The stage needs to be set, the props and costumes put in place, lines learned, and delivery rehearsed. Practice is vital to improve confidence and fluency, and to fine-tune your material for oral delivery.

Getting word perfect

Don't try to be anyone but yourself. Identify your strengths—storytelling or humor—and put them to good use in your presentation. Practice as much as possible. Your audience deserves a presenter who can make the material fresh, understandable, and relevant.

REHEARSE YOUR ATTITUDE

The energy you put into a presentation, and your enthusiasm for the subject, will drive home your message. These apparently natural characteristics need practice, too.

Practicing out loud

Your presentation will be delivered orally, and to reach your confident best, you should practice this way, too. You need literally to deliver your presentation out loud and, if possible, to a test audience that can offer constructive feedback. Run through the presentation in the same (or similar) room or auditorium where you will deliver the real thing, rather than in the car or in your bedroom. Ideally, you should run through your presentation out loud five to 10 times. This sounds like a lot, but the applause you will eventually receive from your audience will make all the effort worthwhile.

Honing your delivery

Your goal is to refine your content to make it as powerful as possible and you comfortable enough with your material to set the script aside. Here are a few practice tips:

- Practice your presentation with an outline, not a full script.
- If possible, practice in front of someone who has knowledge of the material.
- After several rehearsals to help you remember the contents, practice delivering it without stopping in order to judge its flow.
- Time your presentation with each round; make sure to stay on track.
- Absorb your material well enough to give your presentation the look of spontaneity.
- After you are satisfied with the content, try recording a practice round on video. It will give you a new perspective on how you look and sound to others.

With experience, presenters naturally develop their own style of delivery. Some have a talent for keeping an audience engaged with questions or exercises. Others excel at helping an audience understand issues through narrative. No single structure serves all presenters in all circumstances, so it pays to try out many different approaches.

IN FOCUS...
THINKING LIKE A PRESENTER

Growing your presentation skills means thinking like a presenter 24/7. There are many real-life situations where you can develop your skills.

- Practice narrative techniques in casual conversations.
- Identify and follow your natural characteristics when communicating.
- In everyday conversation, watch how your listener responds to different approaches. What works to keep their attention?
- Attend presentations by others. Which styles of presenting keep your attention and which do not?
- Be a collector. Gather anecdotes, stories, and quotes for later use.

- Work on building one skill at a time. Before your next presentation, select one area—narrative skills, or presenting statistics, for example. Concentrate on improving your delivery in that area.
- Get as much feedback from your peers as possible. It is very difficult to evaluate yourself objectively as a communicator.
- Get targeted feedback. Ask someone you know to listen to your presentation with a specific purpose in mind. Tell them in advance, for example, that you'd like feedback on how strong your eye contact is or how many "filler" words you use.

Pacing yourself

Effective presenters know that good timekeeping can be as important as good content. A presentation that starts and ends on time gives a strong impression of competence. Achieving this goal is the result of excellent preparation, making time for rehearsal, and flexibility on the day.

TIP

RECRUIT A TIMEKEEPER

Placing a friendly "timekeeper" in the audience who can unobtrusively signal the time remaining to you is a good way of staying on track.

Preparing notes

A formal presentation or speech is the wrong place for an original thought. Effective communicators plan, prepare, and practice their material. Most presenters use notes. Even if you don't need to consult them, they can be reassuring. Treat them as prompts rather than a script. Write them in the form of bullet points or keywords, not complete sentences, and rehearse "joining up" the points. Don't worry if your words aren't the same every time.

Notes are most useful when they are accessible at any point during the presentation. Use numbered sheets or cards, making sure that your numbers match up with handouts or slides. Your notes can also serve as a backup if you can't use your visual aids.

If you do need to refer to notes, don't try to hide it. Take a moment, review your material, and continue. Your audience will take the pause in their stride.

Timekeeping tips

- Never, ever go over your allotted time. Your audience will thank you.

- Watch your breathing. If you are running out of breath, slow down your delivery.

- If you tend to speak too quickly, try delivering each point to one person, maintaining eye contact with them before allowing yourself to move on.

- It takes about two minutes to deliver a page of double-spaced text.

- When rehearsing, remember that the pace of the actual presentation will probably be slower due to summarizing, natural pauses, and nerves. Compensate by erring on the side of less material, rather than more.

- Don't use automatic scrolling features for projected slides. The presenter, not the technology, should set the pace.

- Practice using a stopwatch. Don't rely on guesswork or estimates.

- If a colleague is going to "drive" the slides for you, practice your timing together so you don't have to say, "Next slide, please."

- Interactivity is an advanced skill, because it complicates pacing. If you use it, consider imposing a limit on the number of questions, or group them together by saying, "I see there are a lot of questions here. If you would, hold your questions and I will address them after this section."

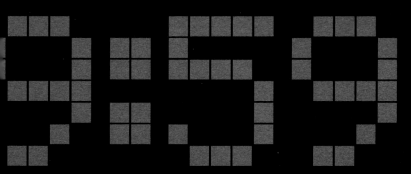

Being spontaneous

Planning for spontaneity appears, at first, to be a contradiction. But building in opportunities to digress from the main path of your presentation allows you to shine in front of your audience, making you appear the master of your material, and so helping retain attention.

Making room for digression

Memorizing your presentation word-for-word is not a good idea. Unless you are a skilled actor, your delivery is likely to be flat and uninteresting. The same goes for reading from a script; listeners may misjudge your authorship, or question your commitment to your words. Instead, practice your material until you know it so well you can deviate from it with confidence. By all means use short notes as prompts, but plan moments into your presentation where you can elaborate on a point of interest, or talk with great passion about an area very close to your heart. Digressions are very useful tools because they can provide "oases"—places where you can take a short respite from the focused intensity of your presentation to talk about topics you know inside and out. These moments will give you a breather and allow you to relax and regain your poise before continuing.

PRESENTING WITH HUMOR

FAST TRACK

OFF TRACK

FAST TRACK	OFF TRACK
Rehearsing your jokes	Forcing humor if it does not come naturally to you
Turning humor on yourself and being self-deprecating	Being sarcastic or making jokes that may embarrass others
Employing humor sparingly to lighten a mood or diffuse tension	Relying on jokes so much your message becomes diluted
Using humor that flows naturally from your own experiences	Using humor that depends on context or detailed explanation

TIP

KEEP ON TRACK
Treat any digression as a chance to connect with the audience. Move from behind the desk or lectern and make eye contact with the audience as you speak. Your audience will perceive your delivery as unique—a presentation tailored to them.

Using levity

Humor can be a powerful icebreaker, and used carefully, will demonstrate that you are attending to your audience because you are sensitive to what they find amusing. If you choose to use humor, be careful how you do so. The wrong joke or story that may have seemed funny at the time can easily backfire and cause irreparable damage to how you are perceived by your audience. The benefits and drawbacks of humor are magnified tenfold when presenting to culturally different audiences: a timely joke will light up the audience and show that you have made an effort to understand their perspective; conversely, an inappropriate joke can be disastrous.

Remember that using humor is not essential, and if you don't feel comfortable being funny, don't try. Similarly, if you have any doubts about the suitability of a joke or type of humor, just leave it out rather than risk causing offence.

Planning the practicalities

The physical environment has a significant impact on the way you communicate and connect with your audience. The success of your presentation depends crucially on whether people can hear and see it clearly. So make sure you consider the physical space in which you will be making your presentation and the equipment you will need.

TIP

CHECK LINES OF SIGHT

If you are using visual aids, consider whether everyone will have a clear view of them, bearing in mind where you will be standing as you describe them.

Assessing the location

The practical side of your presentation demands as much foresight as the content itself. Don't leave the details to others, on the assumption that everyone knows what is required to make your presentation a success. Instead, plan ahead and give yourself enough time on the day to make sure everything is well prepared and make final adjustments. If possible, view the venue and layout (see opposite) well in advance, and arrange a meeting with the facility's manager to request any necessary changes.

CHECKLIST SCOPING OUT THE VENUE

	YES	NO
• Will everyone be able to see and hear the presentation from all vantage points in the room?	☐	☐
• Can you be heard at the back of the room? Take someone with you to help check.	☐	☐
• Can you control the lighting in the room, if necessary?	☐	☐
• Can windows be shaded to eliminate glare?	☐	☐
• Are wall sockets conveniently placed? Do you need extension cords?	☐	☐
• Is there a table for handouts, business cards, or follow-up information?	☐	☐
• Will additional seating be available if needed?	☐	☐
• Will a sound system be necessary for audience questions?	☐	☐
• Is all audio-visual equipment tested and in good working order, and are you sure you know how to use it?	☐	☐

Layout pros and cons

CLASSROOM
The classroom-style layout features rows of seating, perhaps with desks or tables.
Pros: Ideal for larger audiences; desks make it easy to take notes.
Cons: Less conducive to interactivity; people finding or leaving their seats can be disruptive.

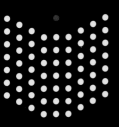

CHEVRON OR WING LAYOUT
This is similar to the classroom style, but the seating is split into blocks angled toward the presenter.
Pros: Audience is brought closer to the presenter; better potential for interactivity.
Cons: Takes more space for fewer seats compared with classroom style.

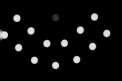

HORSESHOE
Audience members are arranged in curved rows around the presenter.
Pros: Ideal for smaller groups; good for interaction; good lines of sight; provides work space for audience.
Cons: This layout can only accommodate a limited number of seats.

BOARDROOM
Audience members are seated around a long table, with the presenter at the head.
Pros: Generates a sense of formality.
Cons: Some seats have poor lines of sight, making prolonged viewing and listening uncomfortable; showing visuals can be awkward for the same reason.

TIP

ASK FOR QUIET
Before you start, ask for all cell phones and electronic devices to be turned off, and make sure noise from nearby rooms or hallways is abated.

Making yourself heard

If you know you will be speaking with a microphone and public-address system, make sure you arrive early to allow time for a sound check. Your goal is to make sure you will be heard clearly around the room, over the level of normal background noise.

Practice projecting your voice to fill the room's farthest corners without shouting, and without getting too close to the microphone.

Remember, microphones only amplify your voice; they don't improve your delivery. The rhythm, pitch, and expression of your voice need to be as carefully controlled as in any other situation.

Microphone technique

- Don't tap the microphone to test it—speak into it
- Don't get so close that you "pop your P's" or amplify your breathing
- Keep jewelry, hair, and buttons away from the microphone
- Don't pound or tap the lectern or rustle papers near the microphone
- Keep your voice natural and varied
- Do check with your audience, even after the initial sound check, to make sure everyone can hear

Selecting a microphone

Choose the type of microphone suited to the mode of your presentation. Handheld models allow presenters to move while speaking, but limit gestures to your free hand. Clip-mounted, or Lavaliere, microphones solve that problem. Their small size allows them to be secured to a shirt or lapel, and wireless models allow for even greater freedom of movement. However, they must be placed correctly to avoid volume drop-off as you turn your head. Stationary microphones work well if you are using a podium, but limit movement. Whatever your choice, make sure you practice positioning and projection beforehand. On the day, ensure you know when your microphone is on, and how to turn it off.

Using lasers and remotes

Any tool or device that helps audience understanding is worth considering. Laser pointers and wireless remotes have become widely used, and each has its place.

TIP

CHOOSE SIDES

If you are right-handed, stand to the left of your screen or flipchart so you don't have to reach across your own body when pointing. If you are left-handed, stand to the right.

Laser pointers direct a thin beam of light at a screen or other medium. They can be useful for highlighting a particular area of a slide or other visual aid without obscuring the image with a physical pointer.

However, bear in mind that if your visual material is too busy or complicated to be understood without you using a pointer to explain it, there may be a case for simplifying it, or perhaps assigning the various points to more than one slide. If you use a laser pointer, make sure you keep it directed away from the audience to avoid a distracting light show.

Wireless remote controls allow presenters to advance to the next slide without having to stand right next to the equipment. Because this gives you the physical freedom to move around, it can help you achieve the right level of interaction and deliver a professional, free-flowing presentation.

Respecting other cultures

All cultures have their own unique customs and rules, particularly when it comes to speaking and interacting in formal and work settings. While those from outside the culture are generally given some latitude, it is wise to consider any relevant cultural issues before you present.

TIP

GET UP TO SPEED QUICKLY

If you can, get some basic cultural information from your hosts, then supplement your learning with additional resources such as guidebooks and websites.

Knowing the norms

Giving a presentation in a foreign country can be a daunting experience. On top of all the usual issues of preparation, you must deliver your material in an unfamiliar place and setting. However, you can still build rapport with your audience by doing some prior research into basic rules of conduct, or "norms," and how they differ from those of your native culture.

For example, emphasizing points through a strong voice and definitive hand gestures is a sign of confidence in North America. In the UK, however, this style may come across as abrasive—and in China, it could seem vulgar. Passing a microphone over someone's head or pointing to a member of the audience may be perfectly acceptable in Western cultures, but it's the height of rudeness in Thailand.

While direct eye contact is generally valued as a sign of trustworthiness in many Western societies, it is generally considered rude in India and South Asia. Western-style "Casual Fridays," when dress codes are relaxed, may be regarded as unprofessional in other parts of the world. Bare legs for women may be considered normal and practical in some cultures, but unprofessional or offensive in others.

In the United States, Canada, and Australia, the use of first names in business settings is quite common. However, in Hong Kong, Portugal, and Germany, using first names without being invited to do so is considered overly familiar.

ASK YOURSELF... AM I APPROPRIATE?

- What are the proper forms of address?
- What are the appropriate standards of dress?
- Am I aware of any idioms or slang I use? Can I avoid using them while giving a presentation?
- Do I know which hand gestures or body language are appropriate and inappropriate to use?
- Are my visuals clear and simple enough to express my message even if my audience doesn't understand 100 percent of everything I say ?
- Have I run my presentation past a person familiar with local culture before the big day?

Solving problems

Planning for problems isn't negative thinking. It is simply common sense. Consider the industries that devote enormous resources to preparing for unfortunate events they hope will never occur. From airlines to utilities, it is a wise policy to expect the unexpected and arm yourself to handle problems with ease.

TIP

REST UP
Get a good night's sleep before your presentation. This will help you project relaxed confidence.

Preparing a "Plan B"

Even the most carefully crafted presentations will come up against unexpected technical or human problems. Malfunctions in equipment, logistical delays, or lack of preparation on the part of others may conspire to upset your plans. It pays to plan for problems, and have a "Plan B" for every eventuality.

When a problem occurs, you need to act fast. Don't waste time apologizing or fretting out loud about the disruption, just continue as if nothing has happened, by putting your "Plan B" into action.

Always make sure you are one step ahead and have thought of everything. If your computer presentation fails, for example, fall back on the note cards you prepared containing your key messages. Better still, carry an extra laptop as well as a spare projector bulb.

When you rehearse your presentation, identify topics you can leave out if you have been allocated less time than you had expected. Similarly, plan an audience discussion or question and answer session you can quickly and easily deploy if you run short. Your audience will tend to take their cues from you. If you take any mishap or change of plans in your stride, so will they. Displaying a cool head and calm disposition in front of your audience will pay dividends. If there is a mishap, show you are fully in control and you will get right back on track through body language and your words and actions.

Handling interruption

There is usually no need to stop your presentation for latecomers—continue speaking while they take their seats. However, there are exceptions. If a key decision-maker arrives late, pause and provide a quick summary to bring that person up to speed. Make sure it is brief enough that the latecomer does not feel embarrassed. Be ready to handle interruptions of all kinds. The most common of these is the ringing cell phone. If you notice audience members using phones or other electronic devices, others will almost certainly notice, too. Such distractions can quickly disrupt and undermine your presentation.

HOW TO... STOP A PHONE PEST

Request that all phones are switched off before you start.

⬇

If a phone then rings, don't try to speak over it. Pause, let the owner switch it off, and stay calm.

⬇

If the owner picks up the call, pause and wait quietly until he/she has dealt with it.

⬇

If it happens again, call a break and speak privately to the offender.

If you can hear chatter or side conversations, pause. This will draw attention to the culprits who will hopefully realize they are at fault and stop. If they persist, don't single out individuals, but ask firmly if there are any questions the audience wishes to raise. Add that everyone will want to devote their full attention to the next part of the presentation because it contains some very important information.

Recovering poise

There are times when you will find yourself—briefly—lost for words. It can happen to anyone; even actors forget their lines from time to time. Don't panic—you know your material, so skip ahead or summarize what you have covered already: it will appear to the audience to be part of a well-planned delivery. There are tried-and-tested techniques that will buy you a few moments to get back on track. Try one of the following for a quick recovery. Stay calm, and you won't lose momentum:

- Repeat the last thing you said
- Return to a key message
- Pause and review your notes
- Ask the audience if they have any questions
- Use your visuals as a prompt
- Call for a break.

Getting ready to go

The number one strategy for boosting presentation skill is to devote as much time as you can to preparation and practice. Don't take shortcuts. By doing the work in advance, you can make your presentation work for you and communicate successfully every time.

TIP

PRACTICE THE TRANSITIONS

If rehearsal time is short, spend it practicing your transitions from one point to another, rather than delivering details. Getting these moments right will make your presentation appear much smoother.

Making final checks

Run through your presentation perhaps once or twice, either alone or with a "friendly" audience. You are aiming to reaffirm your material, not pick holes in it. You may feel the temptation to rework everything from top to bottom. Resist this urge and stick with the ideas you have developed over time—there is no time to assess the implications of any big changes.

Check your visual aids one last time, making sure you are up to speed with all the practicalities of your presentation. Again, don't be tempted to make any major changes at the last minute.

Speaking at short notice

There may be times when you have to prepare or alter a presentation at very short notice. In this situation, the overriding concern is to use whatever time you do have to best effect.

Focus on your key messages rather than supporting details, and write them into a streamlined one-page outline. Prepare for likely questions, but forget about creating elaborate visuals—you will more often than not get bogged down in layout rather than content. Use existing materials, or do without. When you give the presentation, explain the situation to the audience and offer to answer their questions as best you can, and provide additional material should it be needed.

Am I ready?

ould I deliver this presentation without any
materials or notes if I had to?

Am I confident that I am making my "best case"?

Do I believe everything I am saying?

Is there any part of my presentation I couldn't
fully explain if I had more time?

Have I anticipated any questions I might get?

Have I vetted the information I am presenting
with others?

Do I fully understand my audience's expectations?

Am I ready with follow-up or additional
information?

Do I know what next steps are called for?

Am I looking forward to this presentation or
dreading it?

Chapter 3

Taking center stage

As your presentation approaches, all the preparation you have put into your material and delivery may be overshadowed by the prospect of having to perform. Don't worry. There are plenty of techniques that will give you a real advantage on the day of your presentation, boost your confidence, and help you deal with nerves or mishaps.

Creating a first impression

The first thing your audience will notice is how you look, and this initial impression is hard to shift. Give plenty of thought to the message you want to send through your attire, grooming, and posture. Study yourself in a mirror, and ask colleagues for their opinion on your appearance.

TIP

LOOK SHARP
Change into a freshly ironed outfit just before your presentation (check beforehand that changing facilities are available).

Connecting with the audience

Appearance alone won't win over your audience, but it plays a crucial role in setting out your intent and credibility. When choosing what to wear, consider which outfit will have the greatest influence on the people you would like to impress the most.

For example, if the audience consists mostly of your casually dressed peers, but also includes two directors wearing suits, dress up, not down. If you are the manager of a factory addressing the shop floor, think how differently your message will be perceived if you are wearing a suit or clean corporate coverall.

Dressing to impress

There are no fixed rules about dress and appearance, but if unsure, veer toward tailored, professional, and conservative rather than trying to reassure your audience by "blending in" with their style. You are dressing to create an air of authority and confidence rather than to please yourself, so steer clear of casual clothes like jeans and sweats, leather, shiny fabrics, and anything with prominent emblems or designer labels. Avoid distracting blocks of bright color, though color can be used to provide an accent. Make sure your shoes are clean, polished, and comfortable. If it is painful to stand in them for the length of the presentation, change them.

Minimize jewelry—you don't want your accessories to be the most memorable part of your presentation—and always pay attention to details, even if you won't get that close to the audience. You can bet they will notice if your clothes are wrinkled or your cuffs are frayed. Remove bulging keys, coins, and other loose items from your pockets, and check that your lapels are free from pins.

Whatever your dress, always take the time to groom yourself. Your audience will not forgive an unkempt appearance or poor personal hygiene.

 **ASK YOURSELF...
AM I WELL GROOMED?**

- Is my hair clean, neatly styled, and away from my face?
- Are my fingernails clean and trimmed?
- Have I trimmed my beard and mustache?
- Are any tattoos visible?
- Is my perfume/cologne overpowering? Many people find scent unappealing, so it should be avoided.
- Have I applied antiperspirant?

Looking confident

The audience is on your side. They want you to succeed; they want to learn and be inspired by you. But to win their attention and trust, and to exert your influence, you need to impose your presence and demonstrate confidence in yourself and in your presentation material.

TIP

ACCENTUATE THE POSITIVE

Avoid crossing your arms or leaning backward, away from the audience. These actions send out very strong negative signals.

Growing self-belief

Inner confidence comes from a combination of self-belief and real enthusiasm for your message. When you are confident, you behave naturally, and in the full expectation of a positive outcome. Your self-assurance is genuine and your audience buys into your message.

You can build your confidence over time through exercises in which you visualize success and, of course, through experience. Looking confident and feeling confident may seem two very different things to you, but to your audience, they are one and the same. Employing techniques that make you appear more confident will bring positive feedback from your audience, which will boost inner confidence.

Establishing your presence

TIP

USE PROPS

If nerves deter you from moving your body, hold a prop, such as a pen or wireless remote, in one hand until you find your comfort level and confidence.

You can win the attention and respect of an audience before you begin simply through your posture, and by the way you occupy the space around you. Even if you cannot rearrange the seating in the room, you should become familiar with the room, your position, and the lines of sight—"owning" the space will make you feel more comfortable and confident. Give yourself room to move, and make sure the audience can see your hands. Don't trap yourself behind a desk or use the lectern as a shield—the audience may interpret your position as defensive.

Using body language

If your content is irrelevant or your delivery dull, you shouldn't be surprised if your audience switches off. But they will also disengage if the nonverbal messages you send out are inconsistent with your words. Your stance, gestures, and eye contact must support what you say. In the event of any conflicting information, the audience will tend to believe what your body language appears to be saying.

Start your presentation with a neutral but authoritative posture. Maintain a balanced stance, with your feet slightly apart and your weight spread evenly between them. Keep upright, facing the front, with shoulders straight, not hunched, and your arms loosely and comfortably at your sides. Don't lean on a chair or perch on furniture for support. For the first 30 seconds of your presentation, try not to move your feet. This "anchoring" will help establish your authority with your audience. As you build rapport, you can relax your posture—this will help win you trust and make the audience feel much more comfortable. Leaning forward sends a positive, friendly message.

ASK YOURSELF...
DO I APPEAR
CONFIDENT?

- Is my eye contact strong?
- Am I projecting my voice?
- Am I maintaining good posture?
- Are my hand gestures natural?
- Is my language conversational?
- Are my movements purposeful?
- Do I appear calm and in control?

SPRING-CLEAN YOUR BAD HABITS
Rid your performance of any visible signs of discomfort you may be feeling. Avoid nervous mannerisms such as putting your hands stiffly behind your back, looking down at the floor, playing with jewelry or hair, or fiddling with your sleeves or buttons.

Moving for effect

Human attention is drawn to movement—it is programmed into our genes—so one of the most powerful ways to hold on to your audience, and to make viewers focus on you, is to move.

Always use movement purposefully and intentionally. Merely walking back and forth will be interpreted as nervous pacing and will distract the audience. However, using movement in tandem with your words will boost impact. Here are a few examples where actions will reinforce the message:

• When you want to refer your audience to a projected slide, take a step back toward it, and sweep your arm to guide the viewer's eyes up toward the slide: be careful not to turn your back on your audience as you move.

• Move to a different spot on the stage area when moving from point to point. This can help the audience to separate out your key messages.

• Coordinate your movements to emphasize an important point. For example, walk across the room, and turn quickly to coincide with the conclusion of a point.

Your movements need not be too theatrical. Your goal is to hold the attention of the audience rather than to entertain them.

IN FOCUS...
THE 7-38-55 RULE

According to a study by Dr. Albert Mehrabian of the University of California, how much we like someone when we first meet them depends only 7 percent on what they say. Tone of voice accounts for 38 percent. The remaining 55 percent is down to body language and facial expression. This is known as the 7-38-55 rule.

SHAKING HANDS CONFIDENTLY

ON TRACK

OFF TRACK

ON TRACK	OFF TRACK
Bending your elbow and extending your right arm	Offering just the fingers of your hand
Pumping your hand two or three times before releasing	Holding on to the other person's hand too long or too lightly
Making and keeping eye contact with the person you are greeting	Looking around the room while shaking someone's hand

Using gestures

Use gestures to reinforce points, just as you would in casual conversation; you may need to "amplify" small movements to take into account the scale of a room. For example, a hand gesture may need to become a movement of the whole forearm if it is to be seen from the back. You may need to practice making such gestures appear "natural." Avoid at all costs any intimidating gestures, such as pointing fingers at your audience or banging your hand or fist on the table or lectern.

Many presenters deliberately avoid making eye contact with the audience. But if you can keep your nerve, engaging with the audience in this way creates trust and intimacy and is one of the most effective means of keeping attention, especially throughout a longer presentation.

Unless you are presenting to a very large group, attempt to make eye contact with every member of the audience at least once. Maintain contact for no more than three seconds—longer contact may be seen as hostile. If you find this unnerving, start by making eye contact with someone who looks friendly and approachable before moving around the room.

Remember also to target people at the back and sides, or those who appear less enthusiastic. If you remain too nervous, look between two heads or scan the room. Never avert your eyes from the audience. Not only will you lose their trust, your voice may become muffled and indistinct, too.

Holding the audience

Novelty and expectation will keep your audience focused through the early parts of your presentation. But keeping their attention once they are accustomed to the sound of your voice and your presentation style can be more of a challenge. Watch for signs of disengagement, and be prepared to act quickly to bring the audience back on track.

Keeping interest

You have prepared an interesting presentation. You are delivering it with conviction using a good range of visual materials and rhetorical devices. Yet when you look out across the audience, you don't get the reassurance of attentive expressions on the listener's faces; you may even detect signs of distraction.

Reading signs from the audience

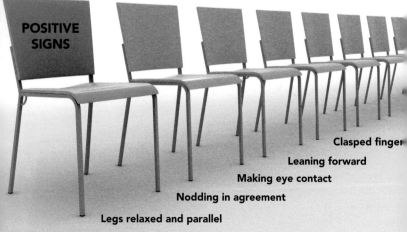

POSITIVE SIGNS

Clasped finger

Leaning forward

Making eye contact

Nodding in agreement

Legs relaxed and parallel

Chin resting on hand

Perhaps your audience is tired, or your presentation is the last in a grueling day, or maybe you are delivering some difficult material. In any case, you need to take action fast:

- **Ask the audience** if they can hear and understand your words and if they are comfortable (it is hard to concentrate in a hot auditorium). Take remedial steps, if necessary.
- **Consciously change** your delivery; slow your pace, or introduce pauses after key points. Change your pitch or volume.
- **Get interactive** and pose questions to the audience and invite answers. Field questions. Leave your position behind the podium and walk out into the audience, making extensive eye contact.
- **Don't get frustrated** with the audience. Compliment them so that they feel valued.
- **Tell your audience** what's coming up, and when: "We'll work through a few examples before moving on to a question and answer session in five minutes." This will help them feel more involved in proceedings.

MONITOR THE MAJORITY

Regularly assess your audience for signs of discontent or agitation, but remember that isolated displays of body language may be misleading, and they can vary between cultures.

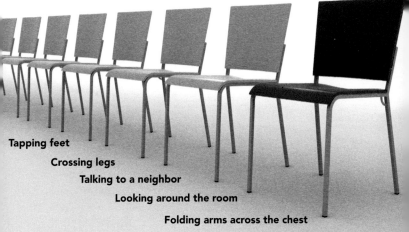

Tapping feet

Crossing legs

Talking to a neighbor

Looking around the room

Folding arms across the chest

Leaning away from the speaker

Taming nerves

Public speaking ranks at the top of many people's list of worst fears. Be assured that this fear is understandable and normal—and even highly experienced presenters sometimes feel some anxiety. Rather than fighting your fear, try to harness it so it works for you. As ever, this requires preparation, practice, and persistence.

TIP

CONTROL THE SYMPTOMS
There are many symptoms of nerves: feeling "butterflies" in your stomach is common, as is dryness of the mouth; twitching eyes; fidgeting or playing with your hair or a pen; and rocking from side to side. Work on controlling the external signs so they are not visible to your audience.

Channeling your energy

Before your presentation, you will be brimming with nervous energy. Start by giving that energy a release: vent any concerns to a trusted colleague, then go for a walk, or do some gentle stretching and warm-up exercises. Your body's physical response to stress tends to work against your mental preparations. Take the following preventative action before you begin:
• Take several deep breaths, holding each for a count of four, then slowly release through your mouth. This will help moderate a quickening pulse and heartbeat.
• Don't take your position too early. Keep your body moving in the moments just before your presentation.
• Shrug your shoulders to help ease tension.
• Give your voice a warm-up by humming; stretch and release your facial muscles.

IN FOCUS...
RITUALS AND CONFIDENCE

Repeating the same sequence of actions and thoughts before each presentation is a helpful tool in preventing nerves. Rituals are used by people to combat much stronger fears, such as agoraphobia and fear of flying, because they set up a safe zone of familiarity. Your ritual can be anything from cleaning your glasses to arranging your papers geometrically on the desk. Just make sure it is a sequence of simple, undemanding tasks that won't cause stress themselves.

Letting yourself shine

Once you begin the presentation, control the release of energy. Don't dissipate it too early by pacing around or rushing your delivery. Maintain eye contact with individuals in the audience; this will help your nerves because it gives you a mental focus, and you will probably get positive feedback from your audience (smiles and nodding heads) that will boost your confidence. Behavioral research has found visualizing a stressful event is enough to trigger a real physical reaction. Conversely, we can all achieve a calmer state through positive images. So before your next presentation, try visualizing your own success.

HOW TO...
VISUALIZE SUCCESS

Imagine yourself taking the stage confidently and speaking well. See yourself enjoying the moment.

⬇

Remember how you feel at your most confident. Tell yourself you can and will succeed.

⬇

Picture yourself as relaxed and prepared—you look more confident than you feel.

⬇

Tell yourself you don't need to be perfect; the audience is on your side.

⬇

Tell yourself you are well prepared. You CAN do it!

Speaking powerfully

How do you sound? In control? Authoritative? Dynamic? Voice is a powerful tool in the presentation arsenal, but don't worry. You needn't have the booming resonance of a stage actor to convince your audience you are fully involved in what you are saying.

TIP

PROTECT YOUR VOICE
Don't drink milk or milk products before speaking—they will coat your mouth. Rest your voicebox (larynx) for at least a day before your presentation, and take regular sips of water while speaking.

Using confident vocals

As you speak, your audience "reads" your voice—its nuances of pitch, volume, pace, and so on. This process happens imperceptibly, below the radar of consciousness, yet it shapes your audience's perceptions of your message. Sound hesitant and your audience will question your content. Sound confident and your audience will side with you. Try using the various facets of your voice (see right) when you practice your presentation and use them to effect.

PACE
Vary the pace of your delivery. This helps keep your audience alert. Speak slowly when delivering key messages—new ideas need time to be processed.

Remaining calm

Slow and deep breathing enhances your performance. It boosts the supply of oxygen to your brain, making you more alert; it helps you stay calm; and it increases the flow of air over your vocal cords, enhancing the clarity of your voice. To keep from stumbling during your presentation, declutter your speech by removing unnecessary words and any trite expressions.

Finally, learn to be comfortable with silence in front of an audience: it feels odd at first, but "dramatic pauses" after key points add memorable emphasis.

Master your voice

VOLUME
Be comfortable projecting your voice so it can be heard everywhere in the room. Vary your projection to grab and keep attention. Your goal is not only to be heard, but also to alert listeners to the importance of what you are saying.

INTONATION
Using an upward inflection (upspeak) at the end of sentences may signal you are uncertain. Using declarative sentences with the voice ending in a downbeat will give even neutral phrases an authoritative touch.

TONE
Whether presenting good or bad information, do so with a tone that matches the content of what you are saying.

DICTION
Enunciate words clearly, adjusting the pace of your delivery where needed. Be careful with acronyms or unusual words your audience might misunderstand. Repeat important numbers for emphasis and to be certain they are heard.

PITCH
Slow your delivery and breathe deeply. Only then will you be able to use the full range of highs and lows of your voice. A confident speaker varies pitch more than a rushed one, whose pitch is flat and unengaging.

Succeeding with formal speeches

Formal speeches such as keynote addresses, appearances at award ceremonies, and addresses to trade conferences and plenary sessions follow structured formats and are often delivered in large group settings. Look on them less as a chance to inform your audience, but more of an opportunity to entertain them, while enhancing your own reputation.

TIP

KEEP DOWN THE DETAIL

There is a limit to the level of detail people can absorb while listening as opposed to reading. Test your speech on someone who hasn't heard it and check that they understand.

Crafting your content

Delivering a formal speech at an official or ceremonial occasion requires a particular method of preparation. Formal speeches may be read verbatim from a script, delivered from detailed cards, or delivered extemporaneously based on careful preparation. However, they lack important features of other presentations. Visual aids are rarely used, and the speaker is physically separated from the audience, limiting the degree of interaction.

As with other presentations, consider the audience and what they need, as well as the messages you want them to receive. Match your delivery to the nature of the occasion. Evening receptions, for example, are not the time for complex content—the audience is more inclined to be entertained.

Without visual aids, handouts, or interactivity, your words must carry the full weight of your message. Keep your sentences short and confine yourself to one point or idea per sentence.

As far as possible, emulate the natural rhythms of speech in your script, keeping your sentences flowing naturally. Although the occasion may be formal, don't fall into the trap of using "sophisticated" vocabulary solely to impress your audience. Instead, use everyday language in a concise and accurate way.

Adapting your delivery style

Even though you will probably be reading your speech, look for different ways in which you can show personality and commitment to your message. Use hand gestures as you would naturally when you speak, to emphasize your points. A simple device like this will help to keep things interesting for your audience.

Don't feel you have to read each word or phrase exactly as written. You should feel free to depart from your speech as required, which will give your delivery a much more spontaneous feel. Aim for a style of delivery that does not call attention to itself, but conveys your ideas without distracting the audience.

- Break up your sentences more than usual so you can deliver them more easily.
- Write delivery reminders to yourself on your script. For example, highlight words you want to emphasize or write in "pause" to remind yourself of pacing.
- Err on the side of brevity.
- Practice your speech until it becomes second nature to you.
- Practice reading ahead so you can speak with your eyes on the audience for as long as possible.
- If someone else has drafted your speech, rewrite or adapt it so that it reflects your own "voice." Add a few personal references to make it seem less formal.
- Visualize yourself as a professional TV host and try to inhabit the role.
- Ask for and learn from feedback.

TIP

Working the room

MAKE IT READABLE

Print out your speech in a large, clear font on single-sided pages. Mark your script for points of emphasis, but make sure you can easily read any handwritten edits or notes.

Speaker podiums give the presenter a place to stand, room to place a copy of the speech, and, sometimes, a stationary microphone. However, podiums can also pose problems. While they do provide some comfort, they also create a physical barrier between speaker and audience, which is a challenge to overcome. Even transparent podiums, designed to mitigate this problem, still force the speaker into a small, tightly constrained space, making it difficult for the audience to gauge their commitment and belief in what is being said.

USING A PODIUM

FAST TRACK	**OFF TRACK**
Placing papers high up on the podium to reduce "head bobbing" as you read	Maintaining a "death grip" on the sides of the podium
Sliding rather than turning pages to reduce noise and distraction	Leaning on the podium
Allowing the audience to respond; pausing to acknowledge applause or laughter if interrupted	Tapping fingers on the podium or near the microphone
Varying voice, tone, and pacing throughout the speech	Allowing your voice to trail off at the ends of sentences
Testing and adjusting podium height before beginning	Turning your head away from a stationary microphone
Standing squarely balanced on both feet at all times	Fiddling with pens, paper clips, or anything else on the podium

To counteract the constraints of a podium, exaggerate your gestures so you can be seen clearly. Use a handheld or lapel microphone to avoid obstructing the audience's view of your face. Plan moments where you can move toward the audience, however briefly, to address a point (question and answer sessions following the speech can offer this opportunity). Freedom of movement will signal your willingness to engage with your audience.

If you are stuck behind the podium, keep in mind you must still find ways to connect with the audience. Make eye contact at points around the entire audience, and find a natural delivery that lets people know the words and thoughts you are speaking are indeed your own.

Using teleprompters

Text-display devices such as hidden screens and teleprompters can avoid the need for a podium. They allow you to appear more fully engaged with your audience by looking in their general direction as you read and delivering your text more naturally.

However, it takes practice to use these devices well. You need to be sufficiently at ease with them, so they aren't a distraction, either to you or your audience.

Follow these simple steps in order to ensure a smooth performance:
• Teleprompters do vary. Rehearse with the actual device you will be using.
• As with every visual aid, make sure you are in control. Be sure to set your own pace of delivery.
• If your script is hard to read in this format, rewrite it. Adjustments now will pay off later.
• Build in and script pauses to sound natural.
• Read ahead in phrases to look more natural.
• Deliberately increase your blink rate in order to prevent "teleprompter stare."

TIP

ACT NATURAL
To make your delivery more human and natural, imagine a member of the audience (or a friend) on the other side of the teleprompter.

Running the Q&A

The question and answer part of your presentation is a great opportunity to drive home your key points and cement the bonds you have established with your audience. Q&A sessions keep an audience engaged and provide you with an invaluable insight into how they have received and understood your communication.

TIP

MAINTAIN OPENNESS

Stay away from defensive language involving phrases such as "You misunderstand my point"—and seek to be empathetic: "I can certainly understand your objections."

Making time for questions

Always allow time in every presentation for questions and answers or some other form of audience feedback. If your format doesn't allow for a session following your presentation, consider addressing questions as they come up.

Audiences often look forward to the question and answer session more than to the presentation itself. It is at this time that their needs move to center stage and they can engage with you directly and test the strength with which you hold your ideas. You should welcome the Q&A because the questions will indicate if you have been effective, and if you have addressed what the audience really wants to know. Consider the Q&A as feedback—a way of strengthening your presentation content and delivery.

Staying in control

Clearly signal the start of the Q&A session not only with your words but through body language; an open posture indicates you are ready for questions. Stay in control of the session at all times by directing the format and focus of the questions. Although this part of the presentation is unscripted, there are techniques to help keep the session focused:

• Keep questioners on track: if they begin to wander off the point, you could say, for example, "We're running short of time and I want to make sure we return to the immediate issue at hand."
• Don't allow audience members to engage in their own separate debates, or to interrupt one another. Step in and direct the process with a quick assertion of control: "Susan, I'd like to hear your question, then we'll turn to the issue Brian is raising."
• Seek to find common themes, or larger points that will get the discussion back to a message: "These are good points that deal with different ways to reach the goal we've been talking about."
• Don't dismiss questions even if it is clear someone missed a key element of your presentation. Graciously repeat a quick summary for the questioner without making them feel awkward.

USE TOUCHSTONES

Keep returning to key words and phrases—or touchstones—in your answers. This will emphasize crucial points and help audience retention.

GOOD QUESTION!

Don't overuse the response: "That's a good question!" or it will lose its meaning with your audience.

IN FOCUS... WRAPPING UP

Signal in advance your intention to close off questions, with a statement such as, "We have time for two more questions and then I'll wrap this up." Don't just end abruptly after the last question is answered. Instead, take a moment to summarize your key points and offer your audience next steps or actions they can take. Be succinct in this final closing, and restate without repeating what has come before. Remember to leave on an upbeat and positive note, and thank people for their time and their attention.

Answering tough questions

Even the most thoroughly prepared presenter will come up against hard questions, or difficult questioners. How you deal with these challenges can win or lose you the presentation because the audience waits to see just how confidently and competently you can defend your position. In many cases, just staying calm and remaining in control under pressure is more important than having all the answers.

TIP

REPEAT THE QUESTION

In larger rooms, when wearing a microphone, repeat or summarize each question for the benefit of others in the audience before offering an answer.

Anticipating situations

It is always easier to appear confident when you have done your homework, and it pays to be well prepared for your Q&A session. Although it is unscripted, you should—with a little knowledge of your audience—be able to anticipate those questions you are most likely to be asked, and those you hope not to be asked. Be ready with suitable answers to both types, but also prepare to be surprised by unconventional questions. No one expects you to have all of the answers all of the time, so don't be afraid to say, "I don't know."

The key to handling difficult questions is keeping your poise. Maintain a calm demeanor, even if the questioner does not. Avoid signaling any discomfort through body language—stepping back from the audience or breaking eye contact, for example.

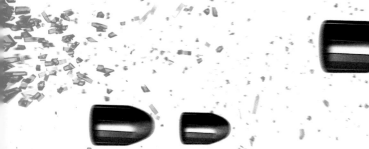

If you have been standing up for the duration of the presentation, remain standing for the Q&A session. Keep a level tone, even if your answer is a candid "I don't know." If caught off guard by a question, buy some time; ask for the question to be repeated, or say that you will need some time to consider and will return to the question later. Even if your audience perceives the question as hostile or unfair, they will still want to see how you handle the response.

Try not to take statements or questions personally, and address the answer to the entire audience while responding. Avoid being provoked and remember, you are in charge of your presentation.

RESPONDING TO QUESTIONS

PROBLEM	SOLUTION	EXAMPLE
Long-winded or unfocused questions	Pose the question differently	"So what you're saying is there's been a lack of progress—is that right?"
	Ask for clarification	"I want to be sure I understand the question. Are you asking why we haven't made progress?"
Skeptical or hostile feedback	Validate the concern	"You're right about this approach carrying some risk, but we can mitigate that risk by the way we handle this."
	Empathize with the concern	"I understand your frustration. This has indeed been a long process. We'd all like to move forward now and get on with implementation."
	Stand firm	"I hear your concern, but let me respectfully disagree with your statement. Here's why."
Questions that stump	Keep your cool	"That's a good question. I don't have the answer for it. Here's what I can tell you though…"
	Return the question	"Let me ask you how you would answer that?" or "Can you clarify why you're asking that question?"
	Delay	"We can certainly discuss it after the session."

Dealing with the media

Media attention carries more credibility with audiences than advertising because it is perceived as being less partial and not paid for. It can help your organization advance ideas or products, and build awareness and credibility with a targeted audience. However, not understanding media priorities can have negative consequences, even for smart businesses.

Understanding your role

Dealing effectively with independent media means recognizing the nature of the relationship you are about to enter into. When you are interviewed, your role is not just to passively answer questions, it is to shape the agenda so you can present your key messages succinctly and effectively. While you can't control the questions asked or the context, you do have control over access and over what you say. Maintaining a balance of control in interviews is a matter of delivering your messages well, through preparation and practice.

Investing in training

Having expertise on a subject doesn't mean you are media-ready. In fact, being close to a topic often makes it difficult to speak in the broad and brief terms media interviews demand. Given that every media interview can impact on your organization's image and reputation, it is worth thinking about investing in training for all managers who are likely to come into contact with the media. Media training provides managers with the means to prepare for interviews, to shape a story through responses to the reporter's questions, and to meet the organization's needs and those of reporters at the same time.

GROUND RULES FOR MEDIA INTERACTION

BE CONCISE AND CONSISTENT
Understand your own message and its context. Be firm when communicating it to the reporter.

EVERYTHING IS ON THE RECORD
Reporters will assume you are aware of this. Anything you say can and will be quoted or broadcast.

AN INTERVIEW IS A BUSINESS TRANSACTION
Set yourself a goal for each interview, then accomplish it as briefly and as memorably as you possibly can. Know when to stop talking.

AN INTERVIEW IS NOT A CHAT WITH A FRIEND
Reporters are focused on getting a story. They do not work for you and will report a story whether it serves your interests or not.

Talking to reporters

Anyone in business is a potential interview subject for a reporter searching for an expert opinion. Whether it is TV, radio, or print media, that opportunity, provided you get it right, can win you a wider platform to gain attention for a product or service, or raise your own profile.

TIP

MAKE INDEPENDENT STATEMENTS

Make sure everything you say to a reporter can "stand alone," that is, make sure your statements are not dependent on a specific context to be understood correctly.

Preparing for the interview

Reporters are always under pressure to produce their stories. You will need to respect their deadlines while allowing yourself time to prepare thoroughly for an interview. Before the interview takes place, ask the reporter for the following information:

• What was it that captured their interest?
• What do they think you can add to the story?
• What approach is being used—do they want a personal story, or a balancing opinion?
• What other sources will they be using—what can you uniquely add?
• Who is their primary audience?

Speaking to reporters under such circumstances, especially about controversial or news-based subjects makes many people worry they will be taken out of context. You can reduce the likelihood of this happening by planning ahead:

• Work your messages into a short, memorable form, using sound-bites for broadcast and quotes for print media. These are what you want the reporter to take away with them.
• Formulate "bridges"—ways of moving between an answer to an anticipated question and a sound-bite you have prepared.
• Seize the initiative by telling the reporter what you have to say about the subject, even before the questions begin. This is your opportunity to influence the direction of the interview.

TIP

FORM CONNECTIONS

Let the reporter know if there are others you are aware of who can provide information or points of view that can aid in understanding. Help the reporter get in touch with those resources.

Getting your message across

A standard line of questioning for reporters concerns the "worst case scenario." Reporters who are seeking interesting comments are prone to press subjects to speculate on what might happen in a given case, which the public might need to know. No matter how carefully phrased, however, speculation is likely to create problems if you are quoted out of context. Replace speculation with an interesting comment on what you do know. You will be in a good position to do so if you understand what the reporter wants and develop your own well-crafted messages to provide it.

BEING INTERVIEWED

FAST TRACK	**OFF TRACK**
Setting a clear goal for every interview	Assuming the reporter will explain your points for you
Taking the initiative in getting your points across	Hoping the reporter asks the right questions
Keeping answers short and memorable	Giving detailed responses and letting the reporter select the relevant parts
Staying focused on your messages and speaking about what you know	Guessing at a correct response or the views of others
Keeping your voice natural and lively	Speaking in a monotone
Anticipating the obvious questions as well as the toughest	Winging your way through and hoping for an easy ride
Correcting any inaccurate assumptions posed within questions	Letting inaccuracies stand

Index

Author Biographies

PRESENTING

Aileen Pincus is the president and founder of the media and communications skills consultancy The Pincus Group, providing training in presentation, media, and crisis communications from offices in Washington, D.C., to clients around the world. She is a former television reporter, having reported at both the local and national levels, a communications director for a US Senator, and a senior executive trainer for a global public relations firm. She is a sought-after speaker on effective executive communication. She lives with her husband Scot and two children, Benjamin and Anna, in Silver Spring, Maryland.

NEGOTIATING

Michael Benoliel is the Director of the Center for Negotiation (www.centerfornegotiation.com). He has provided negotiation training for multinational corporations including Shell Oil, Prudential, British Petroleum, Applied Micro Devices, and PTT Chemicals, in the US, UK, Switzerland, Singapore, Malaysia, Thailand, India, and Hong Kong. Some of his media interviews include: Bloomberg Television; CAN TV Channel 21, Chicago; *BusinessWeek*; *Straits Times*; *The Deal*; *The Washington Diplomat*; The Wall Street Radio Network; WXRK New York; and Reuters. Dr. Benoliel is currently Associate Professor of Organizational Behavior and Human Resources Practice at Singapore Management University. His more than 20 years of academic experience includes teaching effective negotiation in the MBA and Graduate Executive programs at The Johns Hopkins University, University of Maryland University College, and Singapore Management University. He received his doctorate degree in Human Resource Development from The George Washington University and h' doctoral dissertation was selected as a finalist in the Donald Bullock Award. He was trained in the Participant-Centered Learning method at the Harvard Business School. He is also a certified mediator and a certified trainer in Herrmann Brain-Dominance Instrument (HBDI). In 1991, he received the Special Achievement Award from The American Society for Training and Development. Currently, Dr. Benoliel is serving on the editorial board of two academic journals.

Wei Hua is the founder of the management consulting firm International Perspectives (www.international-perspectives.com), and has extensive international experienc in research, consulting, training, and teaching in mainland China, Japan, the US, and Singapore.

SELLING

Eric Baron is the founder of The Baron Group, an international sales and sales management consulting firm. The Baron Group has been training sales professionals and sales managers around the world for almost 30 years, and the concepts included in the selling section of this book reflect much of what is covered in their programs. Eric is an adjunct professor at Columbia University Business School. In 2008, he received the highly prestigious Deans Teaching Excellence Award for his popular course, Entrepreneurial Selling Skills. His first book, *Selling Is a Team Sport,* was published in 2000 and is considered by many to be the definitive book about team selling. The Baron Group's client list includes many international companies including American Express, Research International, Pfizer Inc., JPMorgan Chase, BNP Paribas, BNY Mellon, Deutsche Bank, Prudential, Cadbury, Ogilvy, and Publicis. He lives in Westport, Connecticut, with his wife of 40 years, Lois. His two grown daughters, Andrea and Deborah, have blessed him with three grandchildren.

Acknowledgments

Original editions produced for DK by

cobaltid
www.cobaltid.co.uk
Editors: Louise Abbott, Kati Dye,
Maddy King, Sarah Tomley, Marek Walisiewicz
Designers: Darren Bland, Claire Dale,
Paul Reid, Annika Skoog, Lloyd Tilbury,
Shane Whiting

DK India
Editors: Ankush Saikia, Saloni Talwar
Designers: Ivy Roy
Design Manager: Arunesh Talapatra

DK UK
Peter Jones (Senior Editor), Daniel Mills
(Project Editor), Helen Spencer (Senior Art
Editor), Adèle Hayward (Executive Managing
Editor), Kat Mead (Managing Art Editor), Ben
Marcus (Production Editor), Sonia Charbonnier
(Creative Technical Support), Stephanie
Jackson (Publisher), Peter Luff (Art Director).

The publisher would like to thank Yvonne
Dixon for indexing, Constance Novis for
Americanization, and Margaret Parrish
for proofreading.

Picture credits
The publisher would like to thank the
following for their kind permission to
reproduce their photographs:

8 iStockphoto.com: Steve Dibblee (photo); 8
iStockphoto.com: Bubaone; 10 (icon) iStockphoto.
com: John Boylan; 18 Alamy Images: Pokorny/
f1 online; 20 iStockphoto.com: Suprijono
Suharjoto; 28 iStockphoto.com: Julien Grondin;
32 iStockphoto.com: Eliza Snow; 35 iStockphoto.
com: Jennifer Borton; 38 iStockphoto.com: Mark
Evans; 41 iStockphoto.com: Terry Wilson; 43
Corbis: Klaus Hackenberg/zefa; 47 Corbis: Joel
W. Rogers; 49 iStockphoto.com: Adam Derwis;
50 iStockphoto.com: Roberta Casaliggi; 55
Corbis: Guntmar Fritz/zefa; 57 iStockphoto.com:
Paul Kline; 63 Science Photo Library: Michael
Clutson; 64 iStockphoto.com: Mehmet Ali Cida;
69 Corbis: David Madison; 72 iStockphoto.com:
Cyrop; 76 Getty Images: Tipp Howell (photo); 76
iStockphoto.com: Marc Brown (icon); 78 Getty
Images: Neil Emmerson; 82 (background) Alamy:
Ken Welsh; 82 iStockphoto.com: Clint Scholz; 86
Getty Images: artpartner-images; 88 iStockphoto.
com: Aliaksandr Stsiazhyn; 91 iStockphoto.
com: Floortje; 94 iStockphoto.com: Joshua
Blake; 100 iStockphoto.com: Luca di Filippo;
103 iStockphoto.com: Andrew Lilley; 104 Alamy
Images: Food drink and diet/Mark Sykes; 108
iStockphoto.com: Chris Scredon; 111 iStockphoto
com: 7nuit; 112 iStockphoto.com: Lisa Thornberg
114 iStockphoto.com: Olena Druzhynina; 120
Getty Images: Betsie Van der Meer; 127 Corbis:
Patti Sapone/Star Ledger; 129 iStockphoto.com:
Gary Woodard; 130 iStockphoto.com: Perry Kroll;
132 iStockphoto.com: blackred; 134 iStockphoto.
com: Lise Gagne; 138 Getty Images: Ryan McVay
142 iStockphoto.com: blackred; 144 iStockphoto.
com: Emilia Kun; 146 Alamy images: Swerve; 154
iStockphoto.com: bluestocking; 156 iStockphoto.
com: Rafa Irusta; 162 iStockphoto.com: Tammy
Bryngelson; 165 (background bottom left and
right) iStockphoto.com: Valerie Loiseleux;
165 (foreground bottom left) iStockphoto.
com: Irina Tischenko; 165 (foreground bottom
right) iStockphoto.com: Alexey Khlobystov;
169 iStockphoto.com: Mustafa Deliormanli;
170 iStockphoto.com: Alexandra Draghici;
171 iStockphoto.com: Oktay Ortakcioglu; 176
iStockphoto.com: Clint Scholz; 180 iStockphoto.
com: Matjaz Boncina; 182 iStockphoto.com: Hsin
Wang; 186 iStockphoto.com: bluestocking; 187
(full page) iStockphoto.com: Robyn Mackenzie;
187 (center) iStockphoto.com: Jennifer Johnson;
191 iStockphoto.com: Cristian Ardelean; 194
iStockphoto.com: Mustafa Deliormanli; 196
iStockphoto.com: Leon Bonaventura; 199 Alamy
images: Judith Collins; 201 Alamy Images: bobo;
204 iStockphoto.com: eon Bonaventura; 206
iStockphoto.com: Kristian Stensoenes.